WRITING TO GO

TOP TEN WRITING TIPS

ROB COLTER

D0974000

ANANSI

This edition published in 2009 by
House of Anansi Press Inc.
110 Spadina Avenue, Suite 801
Toronto, ON, M5V 2K4
Tel. 416-363-4343
Fax 416-363-1017
www.anansi.ca

Distributed in Canada by
HarperCollins Canada Ltd.
1995 Markham Road
Scarborough, ON, M1B 5M8
Toll free tel. 1-800-387-0117

Distributed in the United States by
Publishers Group West
1700 Fourth Street
Berkeley, CA 94710
Toll free tel. 1-800-788-3123

All of the stories and examples presented in this book are fictitious, and any resemblance to actual persons, living or dead, is purely coincidental.

House of Anansi Press is committed to protecting our natural environment. As part of our efforts, this book is printed on paper that contains 100% post-consumer recycled fibres, is acid-free, and is processed chlorine-free.

13 12 11 10 09   1 2 3 4 5

Library and Archives Canada Cataloguing in Publication

Colter, Rob, 1945–
Writing to go : top ten writing tips / Rob Colter.

ISBN 978-0-88784-831-5

1. English language — Rhetoric — Handbooks, manuals, etc.
2. Electronic mail messages. I. Title.

PE1408.C64 2009   808'.042   C2009-902833-6

Library of Congress Control Number: 2009929242

 Canada Council for the Arts   Conseil des Arts du Canada   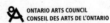 ONTARIO ARTS COUNCIL CONSEIL DES ARTS DE L'ONTARIO

We acknowledge for their financial support of our publishing program the Canada Council for the Arts, the Ontario Arts Council, and the Government of Canada through the Book Publishing Industry Development Program (BPIDP).

Printed and bound in Canada

CONTENTS

INTRODUCTION

You are a recent college or university grad, new to the workforce. Or perhaps you are a more seasoned employee, suddenly required to do more writing than you ever expected. You may be an accountant, an engineer, or a social worker. You may be involved in marketing, banking, or government.

What do you all have in common?

Confronted by a deluge of e-mails, letters, and reports, you lack confidence about your writing ability and find it difficult to complete your best work before the deadline. In fact, you're not sure you could recognize your best work even if you could produce it. As a result, writing is a constant source of stress, and you feel that your messages and documents contain more fizzle than sizzle.

How is it that so many well-educated employees find themselves in this dilemma? The answer is simple: the writing you did in school was very different from the writing you are expected to do in the workplace. The chart below compares the characteristics of each.

Academic	Workplace
Writer-centred	Reader-centred
Single format (essay)	Multiple formats
Broad topic	Narrow topic
Single reader	Multiple readers
Research emphasis	Action emphasis
Long deadlines	Short deadlines
Complex language	Simple language
Length prescribed	Length according to purpose

Of course, essay writing requires analytical and critical thinking, logical organization, and sound grammar and sentence structure. All these skills are applicable to the workplace. But the workplace does not ask you to write an essay of 3,500 words, with a deadline of two months. More likely, you will be faced with 20 e-mails daily to respond to or initiate, several letters that needed to be couriered yesterday, and a report that is due in a day or two.

So much for writing as process! And yet writing is a process, and you cannot succeed at it unless you treat it as one.

This book is designed to give you the confidence to write with greater speed and impact. Speed will allow you to meet deadlines, and impact will ensure that your document is effective. Call it the circle of confidence: you need confidence to succeed, and every success increases confidence.

Writers who lack confidence often think that they are cursed, because they can always point to a friend or colleague for whom writing seems to be as easy as breathing.

If you are a writer who feels the curse, here's what you need to know:

- Writing is not a mystery to be solved, but a process to be learned.
- Writing is a skill, not an inheritance.
- Because writing is a skill, it requires knowledge of certain techniques.
- Because writing requires technique, practice is essential for mastery.
- As with any skill, masters are few, but all can become competent.

Would you expect to become good at tennis if you rarely played it? You can look at writing in the same way. If you lack confidence in something, you tend to avoid doing it, and the avoidance chips away at your ability to perform the task to the degree that it is acceptable or enjoyable to you or to others.

Before you get farther into this book, here's a real-world question for you:

Q: Of the time available for a writing task, what percentage do you spend on planning, writing, and revising?

A: For most writers, a workable breakdown should be about 15 to 20 percent each for *planning and revising* and about 60 to 70 percent *for writing*, depending on the complexity and length of the task.

This means that if an hour is a reasonable length of time in which to complete a particular document, you have about 10 minutes each for planning and revising and about 40 minutes for writing. (This breakdown does not include time for research, should it be required.)

Because purpose and content are situational, these ratios will vary. If you take a few minutes more to plan, you'll probably need a few minutes less to write. If you take longer to write, you might need a little less time to revise. No writing task is ever the same as the last one, but you must give fair attention to each stage of the process.

A young man once told me that he assigned 100 percent of his time to writing, with the explanation that since writing was the task, why waste time with planning and revising. Though his view was extreme, most people do assign too little time to planning and revising. They're anxious to get started. They're unsure how to plan, or they feel they don't have time to plan. They define revision as proofreading — a spell-check followed by a quick scan for obvious errors.

Planning involves *pre-writing.* Revising involves *rewriting.* They are the bookends that support your finished product. If you've neglected to put either one in place, your writing will not be able to stand on its own.

This question of proportion embodies the framework of this book, which is divided into three sections: Think Before You Write; Write According to Plan; Apply Polish. Each section describes specific aspects of the writing process. Examples from workplace settings demonstrate *how* to accomplish your writing goals. Appendix A features examples of documents in which every step of the process has been used. If you apply these techniques to every document you write, the quality and impact of your writing will improve substantially from where it is today.

I have appeared on several television and radio programs, talking about language usage and conducting short quizzes. Most people wince at the very mention of the word "writing," yet when you make a game out of it, they can't wait to give their answer. To stimulate your appetite for the answers, each chapter of this book begins with commonly asked questions, and self-tests are included in Tips Six and Eight. Many chapters also contain anecdotes illustrating problems common to all writers.

It's perfectly understandable that you may feel unprepared for the writing challenges you face in the workplace. Not only were you schooled in a mode of writing that is largely alien to it, but it's difficult to engage in a time-consuming, often solitary process when all around you business is being conducted at speeds measured in gigahertz. Even the word "process," as in "word processor" or "information processing," hints at an industrial rather than a human function.

The goal of this book is to replace this anxiety with confidence, by providing you with the techniques that will enable you to take control of your workplace writing tasks, increasing both the speed and impact with which you complete them.

PART ONE

THINK BEFORE YOU WRITE

Thinking before you write is critical to the success of a document:

- Can you state your purpose in one sentence?
- How much detail does your reader require?
- What is the best format to communicate this?
- What are your main points?
- How do they relate to one another?
- Can you make a point-form outline?

Without this pre-thinking, you will have nothing to guide you as you write.

The process of writing a complex proposal or report is similar to designing and constructing a building. The major difference is that you are the only worker on the job: the design, execution, and completion of the project are entirely in your hands.

This analogy occurred to me while I was working in a sprawling community college that was being extensively renovated, while 7,000 students and staff went about their daily business. As the work progressed, the removal of each barricade revealed a completely altered feature — the most spectacular being a four-storey atrium, accented by expanses of glass and beechwood panelling.

After two years of steady work, the finishing touches were being applied. I was impressed by the smooth orderliness with which this complex project had unfolded. Along a wide, gleaming corridor, laser levels were being used to mark the placement of stringers that would support the ceiling tiles. A foreman was standing by.

"This renovation looks fantastic," I said to him. "How do you keep track of everything?"

"Keep track?"

"I mean, with such an ambitious project and thousands of people milling around, how do you keep everything so well organized?"

He smiled at my naïveté. "It may look complicated, but it's really not," he explained. "All the steps have been planned out ahead of time — we just follow the plan."

Of course. Planning was the key, followed by the systematic application of technique. No wonder he was so confident. He'd done this many times, and he knew it worked every time.

Let's return to our solitary expert, the writer, our one-person construction crew.

In this vital pre-writing stage your goal is to develop a workable plan using no more than 20 percent of your available time.

This represents 12 minutes of an hour.

For short e-mails or memos that take less than five minutes to write, one minute of planning (usually in your head) is probably all that is required.

The chapters in Think Before You Write show how defining your purpose and audience are critical steps in formulating your message. Factors that affect your choice of different business formats are also explained, and the section ends with the final objective of the planning process — the creation of an outline.

Are you a procrastinator? Planning is a procrastination buster. Instead of doodling or biting your nails, you can focus on selecting and organizing in point form the information required by your reader. You can diagram the points you want to make, turning them into a workable outline. This road map will direct you in a straight line to your destination.

KNOW YOUR PURPOSE

"I have trouble getting started."
"I'm never sure when I'm finished."

These statements describe the opposite ends of the same problem: when you begin to write, you need to know what you are trying to accomplish. If you don't know your objective, how can you possibly know when you've accomplished it?

Identifying your purpose must be your starting point. Whether you are responding or initiating, you must be able to phrase your purpose in a single sentence:

- I request that we meet Monday instead of Friday.
- I recommend that we close the manufacturing plant in Dengshu Province.
- We have noticed several inconsistencies in our corporate web site.

You will discover that this single sentence can be used in your introduction or executive summary, or even as the major portion of a short message.

It's amazing how many people avoid taking this simple first step and instead rely on discovering their purpose as they write the document. They may have been taught that such a "free writing" approach is the best way to get started, because it avoids procrastination and engages the writer immediately.

This kind of writing is not "free" at all. In fact, it's very costly, because it wastes precious time. With this approach there is no guarantee that you will *ever* discover your main purpose and, even if you do, it will be enmeshed in a tangle of random thoughts that will take you even more time to sort through.

This is why you need to start with thinking, not writing.

A second reason it is so important to articulate your purpose at the outset is that purpose is inextricably linked to your reader(s) — your audience. Each document you write is custom-designed for a specific *audience* (Tip Two: Know Your Audience). The relationship between *purpose* and *audience* determines how you select and shape the content of your *message* (Tip Four: Outline Your Message).

The interconnectedness of these three factors can be illustrated by an equilateral triangle. For now, we'll label one side only.

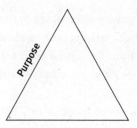

A third reason for knowing your purpose is that your message is intended to influence the reader in a specific way. If you have presented a persuasive analysis, you expect that your supervisor will agree with your recommendation to close the plant in China or make changes that will improve its productivity or reduce its costs. In other words, for each document you write you have an expected outcome.

To stimulate your thinking about purpose, consider your own workplace:

- Can you describe the main purpose of your workplace in one sentence?
- Can you describe the main function of your job in one sentence?
- Check your e-mail and file folders and list the different purposes for which these documents were written. Was the purpose always clear? Do you have any e-mails with a dialogue history seeking clarification?

This inventory will enable you to classify your main reasons for writing both inside and outside the organization. *Your goal is never to leave a reader with a question about what you've written.*

A search through your documents, both as an initiator and as a responder, probably revealed several of the purposes included in the following list. They are arranged in their approximate order of complexity.

- Confirm
- Agree/Disagree
- Question
- Request
- Inform/Report
- Explain/Describe
- Propose/Recommend
- Compare
- Analyze
- Evaluate
- Persuade
- Summarize

Let's look at the characteristics of each of these goals.

CONFIRM

It is unnecessary to provide confirmation unless it is requested.

- I am confirming my attendance at the meeting. (Or "I will be there," or "Confirmed.")

AGREE/DISAGREE

Your agreement or disagreement may be complete or conditional on one or more additional factors. You could capture these differences with the following statements:

- I fully support this proposal.
- I disagree that this is the best approach.
- Although I agree with X, I don't believe that Y will work.
- I can agree with A if B and C are also included.
- I will agree with A if B and C are modified.

QUESTION

Don't hesitate to ask a clarifying question.

- Before we finalize the purchase of X, we have the following questions.
- What years do your statistical data cover?

- Can you please confirm the current list price for product X?

REQUEST

The purpose of a request should be easy to identify, since the request is yours. Still, you have to formulate the wording. You can phrase the request as a question, but you are still expressing a need. Be specific in describing your need.

- Document A-31-40 is missing from the information we received. Could you fax it by tomorrow morning at the latest?

INFORM/REPORT

Generally, the purpose of sharing information is to report progress or changes in projects or systems within your department or organization. Clearly identifying your purpose and staying on message is especially critical if you are addressing a large and varied audience. The last thing you want to do in any situation is confuse people.

Your purpose could be expressed in any of the following ways:

- Beginning April 1 time sheets must be submitted no later than ...

- As we begin Stage 3 of Project X, the following changes in personnel ...
- Please note that Section 02-3-1.1 has been revised to read ...

EXPLAIN/DESCRIBE

You might be asked how something is done in your department, or you might feel it necessary to explain how a certain decision was made in the past. Your purpose is to provide an accurate and detailed explanation. Here are some examples:

- The Policies and Procedures manual is updated monthly. This involves ...
- Before we hired an accounts supervisor, each budget area ...
- The 37 employees in our department occupy 3 common work areas and 6 individual offices in an area of 2,500 square feet.

PROPOSE/RECOMMEND

Proposals and recommendations share common objectives, but there is a difference: proposals present *an offer* for action, whereas recommendations *favour* one action over another, or action over inaction, that will lead to improvement.

Proposals require a lot of research and a persuasive writing style. They make a case for action, which, if accepted, will be followed by analysis. Recommendations follow from analysis already undertaken.

In the business world, proposals and recommendations are considered to be more worthy of attention than suggestions.

What is it, exactly, that you are proposing or recommending?

- I recommend a 25,000-square-foot expansion of our own facilities over the next two years rather than purchasing those of company X.
- We are proposing that we extend all product warranties by one year.
- Because we have greatly expanded our staff, I am submitting a proposal for reorganizing our departmental structure and increasing our office space.

COMPARE

If your purpose is to compare, you will usually consider both similarities and differences, highlighting those that are of particular interest. Comparisons are often made with the use of charts, graphs, or other visual elements such as text boxes. A comparison inherently includes analysis and often an evaluation.

- A comparison of this year's new product launch with last year's reveals . . .
- The cost of using X is higher than the cost of using Y.
- A comparative cost analysis indicates that Y is the better choice.

ANALYZE

Competent analysis is the lifeblood of any successful organization. You may be asked to analyze sales, marketing, or financial data; systems and security operations; organizational needs; client needs; public needs, etc. Analysis involves identifying the parts of a process and examining how they relate. The goal of analysis is to assess whether the process is performing at maximum efficiency. (Evaluation follows from analysis: what is required to bring the process being analyzed to the desired performance level?)

What is the purpose of your analysis? (When it is complete, you will need to say what you conclude from the analysis.)

Let's follow the thinking process involved in this complex activity:

Initial thought:

I have been asked to review the tracking of financial system user accounts.

Revised thought:

> The purpose of the review is to determine whether the system is working as planned.

Statement of purpose:

> I am reviewing *the effectiveness of the methods* we use to track user access to our financial system.

EVALUATE

An evaluation of a process or system can indicate the need for improvement (to increase its value to the organization) or it can indicate the need for replacement. In rare cases, an evaluation can indicate that there is no need for change of any kind.

Although evaluation is often the main goal of analysis, the two are not necessarily performed by the same person. For example, you may be asked to analyze the results of a particular process or project (as in the example above), which your supervisor or manager will then evaluate.

Let's assume that you are in a relatively senior position that gives you the credibility and expertise to evaluate some facet of the organization and report on it.

In this situation, how do you define your purpose?

Initial thought:

I have received the completed review.

Revised thought:

The review concludes that several areas require immediate modification in order to protect system security.

Statement of purpose:

I will evaluate the methodology and accuracy of the review in light of its conclusions and take appropriate action.

PERSUADE

The use of persuasion implies that the reader is not going to be immediately receptive to your message and therefore you will have to frame your position strategically for acceptance. (Framing your message is discussed more fully in Tip Four.) This could take the form of a request or recommendation, where you hope for agreement but have a fallback position if you fail to get it, or it could be in the form of a directive, which you strive to make palatable.

Communication with this purpose is often used in external correspondence, with suppliers or clients or branches of your organization.

If your purpose is to persuade, you could formulate your message in the following way:

Initial thought:
> We need to shorten the shipping time for product X.

Revised thought:
> I've requested this twice in the past two months, but the shippers blame their suppliers for the delays.

Statement of purpose:
> I will offer our shippers an incentive if they can solve the problem with their suppliers.

SUMMARIZE

In the workplace, many writers think of summaries as the recording of notes following meetings or detailed telephone conversations, because these are the discussions they are usually expected to summarize.

As a result, the tendency is to think that these are the only purposes for which a summary is useful.

Summaries involve careful selection of information that will be of value to your reader. This could be in the form of a synopsis of an issue or it could be in the form of background, history, context, or framework of your subject.

Summaries are extremely important in the business environment, which places high value on written documentation that is brief and to the point.

Apart from the heading "Executive Summary," which usually precedes a formal report, summaries can be found in most introductions or background sections, in the body of messages, and often in conclusions. In this sense, summaries are embedded in writing that has a different overall purpose — as part of an analysis or evaluation, for example.

Many organizations require project or trip reports as you near the completion of a project or following a meeting with clients. The purpose of these reports is to summarize the points that are relevant to the reader.

However, it is more difficult to recognize the need for summarizing *within* the body of a letter or report. For each of your major points, you need to ask yourself if a summary of background or context is required.

Direct summaries are usually headed "Meeting Summary" or "Project Summary," which indicates their focus.

Indirect summaries for the purpose of providing background or context could be framed in the following ways:

- A brief look at past practices is instructive.
- Before the acquisition of X, the company consisted of integrated operations at six locations. In 1995 these were reduced to four, and in 1998 to three.

- The recent emphasis on the identification of core values within organizations is an outgrowth of mission statement ideology, which began in the 1980s.
- In summary, the consolidation that the company has undertaken over the past ten years has increased employee morale and productivity.

A FINAL THOUGHT

Without a clear sense of purpose you will meander like an aimless river, turning this way and that, switching back and going in circles. This lack of direction will use up all your available time. You may console yourself that this is your problem, and it won't affect your readers. But remember that your readers have put their trust in you. By communicating to them, you have accepted the responsibility of guiding them to a destination. Would you follow someone without knowing where they were headed or why?

TIP TWO
KNOW YOUR AUDIENCE

- Does audience refer to one reader or many readers?
- What if I haven't met the reader?
- Don't *I* decide what the reader needs?
- Can't I just write for the average reader?

Think about those questions for a few minutes, then consider this story.

Lorraine B.
Lorraine had just graduated from university and immediately been hired by a large insurance company. It was a dream job, with a very competitive starting salary that would only go up and responsibilities that presented a learning curve that would be an education in itself.

On her first day at work, she and several other new hires met with their manager, Susan Lee, who had been with the company 15 years and had received her MBA from the same university as Lorraine. As the new employees learned about their job, Lorraine could easily imagine herself in Susan's position at some not-so-distant point in the future. At the conclusion of the orientation, they were each given a research task and told to submit a one-page report by the end of the week.

"There is no magical formula behind this number," Susan told them. "With 40 people reporting to me, I simply do not have time to read more."

Lorraine took up the challenge with a degree of energy and enthusiasm that went beyond anything she had put into her university assignments. However, by the time she had completed the research and written the first draft, her report was four pages long — and due the next day.

Working late into the night, Lorraine had managed to shorten it to two pages and felt that it could not be shortened any further without rewriting it from scratch. Surely Susan Lee would be impressed at how persuasively and thoroughly she had covered the subject. Surely she would realize that it was unreasonable to limit such a broad topic to one page.

Brimming with confidence, Lorraine dropped by her manager's office first thing the next morning. Handing the report to her, she was hoping to be complimented on her eagerness and capacity for work. Instead, she got the shock of her brief working life.

"I asked for a one-page report," Susan Lee told her. "You have three hours to complete it as directed," she continued, returning the document to Lorraine without as much as a glance at its contents.

Crestfallen, Lorraine went to her work station where, after almost three hours of intense work, she managed to meet the deadline.

Lorraine survived that episode and five years later is now in a position similar to Susan Lee's. A frequent speaker at conferences on workplace communication, she likes to play up the humour in this story and then, when the laughter subsides, underlines the lesson she learned from it: *always meet the needs of your reader.*

Why didn't Lorraine follow Susan's instructions? Because of her university writing experience, Lorraine was used to writer-centred rather than *reader-centred* communication. She focused on her own needs and interests, neglecting those of her reader. *The only time you write for yourself is when you will be the only reader.*

Remember the triangle on page 7? Let's add the label *Audience.*

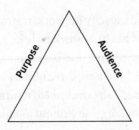

Purpose and Audience are interconnected. Lorraine focused only on the purpose of her report, and thus it was unacceptable to her primary reader.

Once you have written your statement of purpose, you need to consider the characteristics of your audience.

DOES "AUDIENCE" REFER TO ONE READER OR MANY READERS?

Audience can signify one or many readers. It is a helpful word to use because it evokes an image of a speaker addressing an audience of listeners.

Have you ever been asked to address an audience? Probably your first question was "What's the topic?" And probably your second was "Who will be attending?"

You picture yourself in front of a group of people, and you want to feel confident that you will be able to address their information needs. You might not feel comfortable with pitching your ideas to a room of five-year-olds, for example. In other words, you want to be able to match purpose with audience.

The same information applies when you *write* for an audience.

Think of writing help-screen instructions for worldwide users of a word-processing program. As a member of a team of writers, you would personally know only a tiny group of potential users, but you could assume they would be representative of the larger group, since they all have the use of such software in common.

How would you identify their needs? How would you ensure that the help screens are reader-centred? You would conduct pre-release trials, where users at different levels of aptitude use the software and respond to controlled questions.

Marketers test the potential acceptance of new products in a similar way, by hosting focus groups of representative consumers. So do film producers, who will screen a film to a small audience and expose the viewers to different endings to get their reaction before making the final edit and releasing the film countrywide.

These strategies are effective for the mass marketing of products. But the writing you do in the workplace is directed at single or small groups of readers with narrow information needs.

Therefore, there is no point in picturing the average reader, because there is no such thing as the

average reader. Instead, you need to make some educated guesses about your reader(s) and identify the
essential characteristics that distinguish them from
other readers. Once you have this information, you
can create an *audience profile*. (A chart is provided
on page 31.)

CREATING AN AUDIENCE PROFILE

You can build your reader's profile by systemati-
cally answering the questions below. Some of your
answers may be no more than an educated guess.
However, it is important that your analysis be thorough because *you will use this information to select
the level of detail, the type of vocabulary, and the tone
of the language used in your message.*

Question 1:
WHO IS YOUR AUDIENCE?

Your message may be intended for an individual or
a group. If intended for an individual, the contents
of your message are likely to be shared within that
reader's working group. Thus, you need to know
both your primary and secondary readers. In large
organizations it is not uncommon to experience a
change in supervisors every year. *If this individual
is your primary reader, it is very likely that you will
have to adapt your communication strategy for each
reader.* (See example 2 on page 33.)

Is Your Audience Internal or External?

Are you writing for readers inside or outside your organization? If you haven't communicated with them before, likely it will be easier to get information about them if they are fellow employees.

External communication is often more formal in tone, since the relationship is more remote and the business is between companies, not individuals within the same company. You should treat every instance of external communication as a public relations opportunity for your organization — in the minds of your audience, *you* embody the organization, and what you say and how you say it reflects its image.

What Is the Relationship of Your Audience to You?

What is your reader's job title? What is your relationship? The answers to these questions will influence the language level and the *tone* of your message.

Picture some people at different levels in your organization. It is immediately obvious that you would not write to each of them in exactly the same way, just as you don't speak to them in the same way. Some require detailed explanations, even about how you spent the weekend, while with others you have to work hard just to maintain their interest. You use an informal tone and vocabulary with some but choose your words more carefully with others.

Upward communication to a superior generally requires more formal language than *lateral* communication to a peer or *downward* communication to a subordinate.

Purpose and audience also play a role. For example, a fundraising letter will describe the seriousness of the issue for which the funds are being sought, but the tone of the letter will appeal to a broad spectrum of readers.

Formal language does not contain contractions (*doesn't*) or slang (*awesome opportunity*) or idiomatic expressions (*when all is said and done*). For these reasons, one might describe the tone of this writing as reserved. It is important to note that a reserved tone isn't an unfriendly tone. The more serious or complex the subject, the more formal the language used. External communication generally uses more formal language, because the writer's relationship with the reader is at arm's length.

Informal language documents are equally concerned with the message, but they also establish rapport with the reader by using a more conversational tone and a less formal (though precise) vocabulary. As noted above, informal language is most commonly used in e-mails for internal communication between peers. (See Tip Three on Formats and Tip Six on Sentences for related information.)

How Does Your Audience View Itself?

Some audiences take themselves and their work very seriously. For example, law courts implement very strict codes of conduct to ensure order and decorum. Such levels of formality and tone are sometimes referred to as corporate or organizational culture.

How do the members of a particular audience situate themselves in society? How do they expect to be addressed? What might they consider to be inappropriate?

If you were in charge of planning a public relations event for YouTube, and on the same day another for the Architectural Design Association, you would quickly realize that you are dealing with two audiences who have very different expectations of what is appropriate.

Within your own organization, compare how the Accounting Department and the IT Department view themselves. Very differently, I'll bet.

Have You Written to This Audience Before?

If you have had previous communication with your audience, you have some feel for the nature of your interaction. Did your readers respond as you expected, or was their response more formal than your original tone? Did they have further questions? Perhaps they expressed their appreciation to you. You should retain this information for the next time you communicate with them.

Question 2:
WHO ARE *YOU?*

This may sound like a silly question. But does your audience know *your* characteristics? Can they believe and trust in what you say? What gives you the authority to write to them in the first place?

For those inside your organization, your credibility is automatically established by your job title. For those outside your organization, this assurance may require more detail.

No matter the relationship, you still have to make a solid case for your credibility, and in some situations it will be helpful to summarize your relevant experience or the depth of your research into the subject at hand.

Question 3:
WHAT DOES YOUR AUDIENCE
KNOW ABOUT YOUR SUBJECT?

You may not know for certain how much members of your audience know about the subject you will be addressing, but you can make an educated guess by noting their titles, their years with the organization, your previous correspondence with them, articles or reports they may have authored, or their reputation in the field. Are they experts in your subject or novices? Google searches can provide useful information, if the sources are reliable.

You need to know your audience's grasp of the subject in order to determine how much detail to provide and at what technical level. Will they need background?

What *Don't* They Know?

Identifying what information your audience *doesn't* know is sometimes easier to determine than what they *do* know. Filling this gap in their knowledge might be your very purpose in writing to them.

Resist the temptation to display too wide a grasp of the subject. *Stay focused.* Writers who don't resist may begin their document too far back in history, add interesting but irrelevant comparisons, or include more details than are necessary for that particular reader.

What *Do* They Need to Know?

Of course, this is your reason for writing. If you have compiled thorough answers to the two previous questions, you should be able to answer this question with precision.

Question 4:
WHY DOES YOUR AUDIENCE NEED TO KNOW THE INFORMATION YOU ARE PROVIDING?

This question should be asked more often, because it defines your purpose for writing. If they asked for the information, presumably they've explained their reasons. If you're initiating the document, presumably you've given this question adequate thought.

Are They Likely to Be Receptive to Your Message?

At this stage of your audience analysis, the level of receptivity should be clear and you can formulate your message accordingly. (See Tip Four)

What Is the Best Format to Communicate Your Message?

Choosing a format depends largely on the nature of your message. If simple and informal, e-mail is likely the best choice. If more complex and lengthy, letter or report format would be necessary. If you have corresponded previously with this reader, he/she may prefer a particular format, in spite of what you think is most suitable.

Question 5:
WHEN DOES YOUR AUDIENCE REQUIRE THE INFORMATION YOU ARE PROVIDING?

If research or collection of material is required, you should gather what you need before you begin to plan the writing of your document so that you can accurately apportion your time.

KNOW YOUR AUDIENCE ◄ 31

These questions can be answered in a few minutes and the information entered on an Audience Profile Chart, shown below.

Audience Profile Chart

Date_____   Purpose: (one sentence)_____

Deadline_____

Primary Audience Identity_____

Secondary Audience Identity_____

Internal_____

External_____

Superior_____   Subordinate_____   Peer_____

Audience Self-View

   (reserved/outgoing, intellectual/practical, etc.)_____

Previous Correspondence_____

Your Credibility in Relation to Your Purpose_____

Research Required_____

Audience Knowledge of Subject:

   High_____   Low_____

Gaps in Essential Knowledge_____

Must Know_____

Why?_____

Receptivity_____

Best or Preferred Format_____   Length_____

Document Characteristics

Level of Detail: High_____   Low_____
Vocabulary Level: Expert_____   Layperson____
Language Tone: Informal_____ Formal_____

While this can seem like a lot of information to compile, it won't take more than a couple of minutes to complete the chart. It gives you a systematic way of assessing your reader's needs so that you can select content and an appropriate level of language. It can even help you to improve routine e-mails and form letters.

Treat it as a thinking tool and it will be worth the effort.

ADAPTING CONTENT FOR DIFFERENT AUDIENCES

A clear sense of purpose and a clear understanding of your reader's needs enable you to custom-design your message to suit a specific situation. If you change your purpose from *inform* to *persuade*, you will need to construct your message differently. Similarly, if you are writing to a different reader, you need to modify your message to take into account that reader's relationship to you and your subject.

EXAMPLE 1

Senior management has decided to acquire the assets of the company's main competitor. Since management needs the approval of the company's Board of Directors, the managers submit a report outlining their reasons in detail, backed up by hundreds of pages of financial analysis and strategic repositioning scenarios.

These details will not be shared across the organization. Instead, the Communications staff will confer with senior management and issue a one-page memo to all other staff, outlining the background and the main benefits of the decision for all employees.

Two messages on the same subject, but tailored for two different audiences.

EXAMPLE 2
First Scenario
You are one of 12 branch managers of Continental Bank reporting to Sabrina Singh, Administrative VP for your sector.

Your Purpose
To get approval to offer new mortgage purchasers a discretionary rate reduction of up to 2 percent.

Audience (Reader) Characteristics
You have reported to Sabrina Singh for three years. She is extremely competent and an excellent communicator. Though she plays by the book (like all good bankers), she welcomes proposals that increase branch identity, but she expects a solid rationale backed up by achievable outcomes. She prefers to communicate by e-mail, wants you to get to the point immediately, and places a high value on clarity of vision.

Since you already know her profile, you can shape your e-mail appropriately.

You Get Straight to the Point

I am requesting your approval to offer new mortgage purchasers a discretionary rate reduction of up to 2 percent.

You Provide a Rationale

As you know, the housing market in our service area has skyrocketed in the last six months, and there is huge potential to increase mortgage sales to new customers. Fifty-six homes were purchased in the spring quarter just ending, and a 20 percent increase is forecast for the summer quarter, and possibly higher in the fall.

You Outline Your Proposal

We have always had the discretion to offer up to 1 percent incentive to new buyers but, given the anticipated volume, a further 1 percent would give us the opportunity to increase sales and build our client base for the long term, as this neighbourhood is experiencing a generational change.

Currently, our new mortgage sales are running 10 percent ahead of last year's, and I expect that this incentive would give us another 5 percent increase.

You Provide Backup

The attached spreadsheet displays our mortgage transactions by quarter YTD and projects the next two quarters, assuming 0.25 percent increments up to 2 percent in summer and fall of this year.

You Close

Thank you for your attention to this request, and I look forward to your feedback.

Second Scenario

The VP, Tony DaCosta, is new to the organization and you've had little communication with him so far.

How does this affect your proposal? A whole lot. Your purpose hasn't changed, but you know very little about your reader's likes and dislikes. He was introduced at a managers' meeting when he replaced Sabrina Singh (who was promoted to a more senior position) two months ago. He stated then that he was satisfied with the status quo and requested patience as he gets to know each of the branches over the next six months.

You phone a few fellow branch managers and piece together the following information.

Audience (Reader) Characteristics

Tony DaCosta appears to value corporate identity over community, in spite of what he said at the meeting. He has not initiated an e-mail to you or any of your colleagues, and his e-mail responses to their routine questions have been short and impersonal. It seems that he is waiting to receive your first quarterly reports, due in a month, before discussing each of your operations.

From this scant information you conclude the following:

1. Before you state your purpose, by way of context you will have to provide brief details of your successes over the past three years.

2. You will have to persuade him that community identity is extremely important to the success of your branch.

3. You will provide him with the same rationale and proposal details as you would for Sabrina Singh, with two differences: it is here that you will state your purpose, instead of at the outset, and instead of attaching the spreadsheet, you will mention only that you can provide sales figures and trends if he wishes to see them.

4. Given that you will have included more information in this message, you might consider sending this as a written memo via interoffice mail, especially since Tony DaCosta doesn't seem accustomed to using e-mail.

Why wait so long to state the purpose? This VP needs to know the relevant facts about your operation before you reveal your proposal. You need to offer some persuasive evidence that will help him understand why your proposal has merit. Although you had earned the trust of Sabrina Singh, now you must start over with this new VP.

In addition, starting with an assertive proposal might seem pushy in these circumstances. You don't have any communication experience with Tony DaCosta. You want to sound him out on your idea, but you don't want to come on too strongly. You're tiptoeing to some extent, giving him the opportunity to know how you view your branch role and to respond to your proposal. You let him know that you've got the backup spreadsheet, but leave it up to him to decide when and if he wants to see it.

EXAMPLE 3

You have purchased an electric pencil sharpener and are surprised that it contains operating instructions, as follows:

Sharpening Pencils

1. Insert the plug into any standard 120 volt AC outlet.
2. Insert the pencil into the sharpening hole and firmly press downward. The automatic switch will turn the sharpener on.

3. After two to four seconds, remove the pencil as the sharpener will have automatically sharpened it.
4. Pull out the pencil.

Emptying the Pencil Shavings

1. Remove the plug from the outlet.
2. Slide the shavings' receptacle out of the main unit.
3. Empty the shavings' receptacle.
4. Slide the shavings' receptacle back into the main unit.

What assumption has the writer made about the intended users of this device? What changes would you make if you were the writer? (See page 203 for feedback on these questions.)

Having analyzed your purpose and audience, you now know your information goals and have a clear picture of your reader's needs. However, you may be uncertain of the most effective format. For example, you may be torn between writing an e-mail and sending a printed memo through interoffice mail. Choosing a format is a decision that you must make before you attempt to create an outline for your document.

SELECT YOUR FORMAT

William H.

"I tend to use e-mail for everything, so I have trouble deciding which layout or structure I should use when I'm asked to write a letter or report."

Think of format as the packaging in which you wrap your message. Just as you adapt your message for a specific purpose and audience, you select the format that best suits its scope, content, and degree of formality.

LEVELS OF FORMALITY

- *Paper documents* are considered to be more formal than electronic documents.
- *Memo format* (especially e-mail) permits informal language, as do some e-mail letters, depending on the purpose and audience.
- Where *privacy and confidentiality* are a concern, documents are normally delivered in paper form.

- *Reports, proposals, and minutes* all use a formal level of language. (See pages 24 to 27 for details about language levels.)

Business writing is results-oriented. Clarity, precision, and conciseness are of the utmost importance. Communication formats are designed to help the writer stay on focus and to help the reader easily digest the information.

This chapter focuses on the design and uses of the six most common types of business correspondence — e-mail, memorandum, letter, proposal, report, and minutes, in both their electronic and paper versions. Examples illustrating these formats are provided in Appendix A.

Many organizations and professional bodies provide templates for all their writing needs, including specialized documents such as sales letters, assessments, or advisories. Although these documents vary in their emphasis and organization, they can be classified under the five general formats noted above.

When in doubt about which format to use, look around you. What formats are your co-workers using? Who does work that is most similar to yours? You are not likely to be the first person to have asked this question, and someone nearby will have the right answer.

FORMATS

E-MAIL

E-mail (or *email*) is both a memo format and an *electronic medium*. Letters, proposals, short reports, and minutes can all be distributed via e-mail, either in the body of the e-mail or as a document attachment. (Faxing is also an extremely useful electronic medium for all these formats, not only ensuring an instant paper copy, but a signature as well.)

The appeal of e-mail is obvious. You don't need a printer, paper, or envelope, and the completed message is delivered instantly and effortlessly. Yet it is not a suitable medium for all messages.

When using e-mail for business communication, all conventions of standard English usage apply: complete and grammatically correct sentences, correct spelling and punctuation, appropriate tone, effective organization and layout — and no short forms commonly used for text messaging.

Still, e-mail is a friendly medium, somewhere between a telephone call and a printed message, and the tone is often informal and conversational.

MEMORANDUM (MEMO; MEMOS)

Memos are used for short, informal messages. The memo form is the most widely used format in business and is the template used for e-mail. Its simple design assists both writer and reader by establishing focus and encouraging brevity. The headings address the essentials and the text follows.

Memo: E-mail Format

E-mail memos should be limited to two screens or less. If longer, attach your text as a file. Headings are supplied.

Sending	Receiving
To:	From:
Cc:	Date:
Subject:	To:
	Subject:

When responding, many choose to use the *REPLY* feature, which can provide a useful record of the correspondence. But keep in mind that, should you want to share the most recent message, the entire exchange will be included. All this repeated information will also place an unnecessary burden on electronic storage capacity. Avoid using *REPLY ALL* unless specified for project consultation or online conferencing.

Cc: (Carbon Copy)

Think before you use this feature. Unless your message provides general or group-specific information, such as an announcement or minutes of a meeting, your reader might consider your correspondence to be private or privileged.

Who *requires* a copy from you? What will be *the specific benefit* to them?

Everyone in business complains about receiving too many e-mails, and the unnecessary use of this feature, along with *REPLY ALL*, is one of the main reasons.

Subject

In the subject line it is important to capture the specific nature of your message in as few words as possible. What is the focus of your message?

For example, *Meeting* is too vague. Choose *Meeting Date* or *Minutes of Meeting. Budget* is also vague. Add *Update, Surplus,* or *Review.*

An accurate subject line will help the reader locate this e-mail in the future. *Never* send an e-mail with an empty subject line.

Salutation: An e-mail memo can begin with a friendly greeting, followed by a comma or dash:

Hi Rebecca,
Good morning, Richard —

Purpose or Main Point: Get to your main point immediately. Do not repeat the subject line. (Many e-mail messages are no longer than a sentence or two, so that everything can be said in the opening.)

Background (If Required): Provide context or a brief history of events or decisions.

Body: Supporting points and detail (if required).

Concluding Statement (Often Expressed as an Action): Make it clear what is expected of the reader. A puzzled reader is a reader whose time you have wasted.

Complimentary Close: *Regards* is a standard closing, followed by a comma, then a space and your first name or, if you have not met or corresponded previously with the reader, your full name.

Depending on the context, you could also end with a continuity statement such as "I'm looking forward to meeting you next week."

Some writers capitalize on e-mail's directness and brevity by choosing not to include either a salutation or a complimentary close. Others find this approach abrupt and unfriendly (although this has always been the practice with paper memos). The difference is in the medium: an e-mail memo is less formal than the paper version.

Memo: Paper Format

Memos are used for short, informal messages within the organization. Choose paper when the memo is to be attached and circulated with other printed materials, or when it contains confidential information.

Use your company's memo format (this can be a customized template with logo) or choose a plain version from your word-processing software.

The date is often placed first. *No salutation or complimentary close is included,* which adds to the formality of the paper version.

(COMPANY NAME AND LOGO)

MEMORANDUM

To:
From:
Date: (often placed before *To*)
Subject:

Purpose or Main Point:
Background (if required):
Body: supporting points and detail (if required):
Concluding statement (action):
(Sender's Initials)

Copy to: (receivers' names: sometimes given as Cc: after *Date*)
Attached: (identifies the document the memo accompanies)

If the memo ends at the top of the second page, adjust the layout to fit all your text on one page, or increase white space to justify using two pages. You do not want to create a second page that begins with your initials or the last line of the body.

LETTERS

Letters are used for external communication when your purpose requires a general mail-out, no matter your subject or audience — for example, a billing, an advertisement, a survey, or an invitation. Not everyone uses e-mail, and a piece of paper in the hand can also have more impact.

Letters are also used for official, legal, medical, and financial correspondence, and for all occasions when confidentiality and security are essential.

E-mail letters are often used as a transmittal device, for example to notify the recipient that a letter has been mailed or to quickly obtain non-confidential information pertaining to an ongoing correspondence (such as between lawyer and client).

Some organizations require supervisory approval before paper letters are sent, a policy that underlines the greater care expected when using this more formal medium.

Letter: Paper Format

There are four common letter styles: *block, simplified,* and two versions of *semi-block.* Because business stationery begins with a letterhead that can be situated anywhere across the top of the page, block style is preferred. The letter on page 50 is an example of block style.

Simplified style has gained some ground, but old habits die hard, and most writers still prefer to begin with a salutation and end with a complimentary close.

No matter which style you use, the content of the body is arranged in the same way and the paragraphs are separated by a single space or indentation.

The components of a standard business letter are as follows (note that the bolded headings below are not used in the letter):

Heading: company name and address, or letterhead

Date: M, D, Y **or** D/M/Y

Name and Address of Receiver

Salutation follows two spaces below. This could be Dear (first name); Dear (last name, prefaced by Mr. or Ms.); Dear (first and last name); or Dear (Sir, Madam, or title, when name is unknown to you). An Attention Line is often used in place of this last example. (*Attention: Accounts Payable*)

In formal letters, a colon follows the salutation; in less formal letters, a comma.

The Subject Line is placed two spaces below and sometimes abbreviated to **RE:** which states the purpose or main point. (In simplified style, no heading is used.)

Purpose or Main Point

Background (If Required)

Body may contain one paragraph of supporting details or several paragraphs, each containing a main point and supporting details. Headings may be used to signal separate sections.

Concluding Statement is the final sentence or paragraph, which indicates expected action.

Complimentary Close: *Yours truly, Yours sincerely,* or *Sincerely,* followed by a comma and your signature on the next line.

Signature Block
Your full name is placed below your signature, followed on the next line by your position title and

on the next line by your address, if this information was not included in the heading.

The typist's initials (let us hope that you have a skilled typist!) are followed by Enclosure (no punctuation), should there be one, and cc., should there be any other recipients, with the inclusion *By fax, By mail,* or *By courier.*

Block Style

The distinguishing feature of block style is that all lines, including headings, addresses, salutation, message text, and closing, begin at the left margin. Today this style is often called letterhead block, in recognition of the non-conforming placement of the letterhead.

Maple Tree Trust
139-15th St., Brandon, MB R7A 6C4
(204) 111-1111 • www.mapletreetrust.com

March 1, 2006

Mr. Winston Fei, Director
Northland Foods
22 Trailway Road
Bridley, MB R6A 5D5

Dear Mr. Fei:

Thank you for your recent inquiry regarding expansion of services to business clients in Bridley and surrounding areas.

Your business is important to us and we are committed to providing the highest possible level of service to each member of the Bridley business community.

At the end of this month Maple Tree Trust will be announcing a major expansion of services, which will reflect all of the input received from business clients such as you.

Thank you for your valuable contribution to our continuing commitment to service excellence.

We look forward to serving you in the near future.

Yours sincerely,

Julia Baumgarten
Client Service Associate
Maple Tree Trust

JB:kh

Simplified Style

Here the salutation and complimentary close are omitted, and the subject line is written in upper or title case. Simplified style is essentially memo format applied to a letter.

Maple Tree Trust
139-15th St., Brandon, MB R7A 6C4
(204) 111-1111 • www.mapletreetrust.com

March 1, 2006

Mr. Winston Fei, Director
Northland Foods
22 Trailway Road
Bridley, MB R6A 5D5

Expansion Announcement

Thank you for your recent inquiry regarding expansion of services to business clients in Bridley and surrounding areas.

Your business is important to us and we are committed to providing the highest possible level of service to each member of the Bridley business community.

At the end of this month Maple Tree Trust will be announcing a major expansion of services, which will reflect all of the input received from business clients such as you.

Thank you for your valuable contribution to our continuing commitment to service excellence.

We look forward to serving you in the near future.

Julia Baumgarten
Client Service Associate
Maple Tree Trust

JB:kh

Semi-Block Style

This style is well-suited to non-letterhead stationery. The sender's address, the date, complimentary close, and signature begin two spaces to the right of centre, giving a balanced appearance to the top and bottom of the page. Use of a subject line is optional.

Maple Tree Trust
139-15th St., Brandon,
MB R7A 6C4
(204) 111-1111

March 1, 2006

Mr. Winston Fei, Director
Northland Foods
22 Trailway Road
Bridley, MB R6A 5D5

Dear Mr. Fei:

Thank you for your recent inquiry regarding expansion of services to business clients in Bridley and surrounding areas.

Your business is important to us and we are committed to providing the highest possible level of service to each member of the Bridley business community.

At the end of this month Maple Tree Trust will be announcing a major expansion of services, which will reflect all of the input received from business clients such as you.

Thank you for your valuable contribution to our continuing commitment to service excellence.

We look forward to serving you in the near future.

Yours sincerely,

Julia Baumgarten
Client Service Associate
Maple Tree Trust

JB:kh

Semi-Block Style Paragraphs Indented

This style is identical to the semi-block style, except that the paragraphs are indented one tab, further opening up the text.

Maple Tree Trust
139-15th St., Brandon,
MB R7A 6C4
(204) 111-1111

March 1, 2006

Mr. Winston Fei, Director
Northland Foods
22 Trailway Road
Bridley, MB R6A 5D5

Dear Mr. Fei:

Thank you for your recent inquiry regarding expansion of services to business clients in Bridley and surrounding areas.

Your business is important to us and we are committed to providing the highest possible level of service to each member of the Bridley business community.

At the end of this month Maple Tree Trust will be announcing a major expansion of services, which will reflect all of the input received from business clients such as you.

Thank you for your valuable contribution to our continuing commitment to service excellence.

We look forward to serving you in the near future.

Yours sincerely,

Julia Baumgarten
Client Service Associate
Maple Tree Trust

JB:kh

Letter: E-mail Format

E-mail format dictates the layout. Limit e-mail letters to the situations noted at the beginning of this chapter.

Write an e-mail letter the same way as you would a paper letter, including the salutation and placing your signature block *after* the complimentary close.

This is analogous to the common practice of attaching your business card information to the end of an e-mail.

PROPOSALS AND REPORTS

Depending on their length and their audience, proposals and reports can be written in different formats. Short proposals or reports are three to five pages long and are often referred to as *informal,* or *memorandum,* reports.

	Internal	External	Format
Short (Informal) 3-5 pages	X		memo
		X	letter
Long (Formal) 6+ pages	X		separate doc. with cover memo
		X	separate doc. with cover letter

This book does not include examples of long proposals or reports.

Short Proposals

A marriage proposal is more than a suggestion, and business proposals must be just as carefully considered.

Longer proposals are often submitted in response to Requests for Proposals (RFPs) issued to outside providers by governments and other large organizations. These are usually referred to as formal proposals and can be hundreds of pages long. Longer proposals include a table of contents, list of illustrations, and citations.

Short proposals are used when responding to a client's request for services, or within an organization to explore or recommend a business opportunity. When appropriate, short proposals can also be written without using memo or letter format. Although less than five pages long, the example in Appendix A is written as a separate document with a cover letter (or *letter of transmittal*) because it is attempting to secure government funding for a project initiative. Memo or letter format would interfere with the organizational structure of the submission.

Because your goal is to persuade the reader to accept your proposal, the information must be complete and accurate. Long or short, proposals must provide specific information, signalled by headings:

Introduction: Brief summary of proposal and its rationale; start and completion dates; your qualifications (if unknown to your reader); proposed methodology.

Background: Current situation that proposal is intended to address; relevance of proposal.

Proposed Plan (Including Methodology): Goals and detailed proposal description (*What* and *How*), with section headings.

Budget: Costs, including personnel and materials.

Timeline for Implementation and Completion: Weekly.

Whether long or short, proposals can be submitted on paper or by e-mail as a PDF attachment. In the latter case, e-mail becomes the letter of transmittal. The proposal example in Appendix A is short but because of its purpose is treated as if it were a formal proposal.

Short Reports
Like short proposals, short reports are generally five pages or less. Their purpose can be informational or analytical. They could be used to report the progress of an ongoing project, the results of an income tax

audit, recommendations following an evaluation, or the findings of an investigation, for example.

In contrast, long (formal) reports can be book-length, with title page, table of contents, background and summaries, introductions, a detailed body with hundreds of subsections, ending with conclusions, recommendations, and appendices. A company's annual report is an example of a formal business report. The NASA investigations of the two space shuttle disasters are examples of formal technical reports (and worth looking at).

A one- or two-page report is often called a *Memorandum*, or *Letter Report*, because its length and purpose suit those formats.

Short reports can feature different headings, but all contain the following basic elements:

Introduction: "In 2002 an oversight system was implemented to deactivate user accounts within 24 hours of an employee's departure from the company. This report analyzes the status of 25 user accounts assigned to now-terminated employers."

Summary: "After presenting the results of the investigation, the report recommends a review of the oversight system under the direction of the senior manager, IT Systems."

Findings: "Three of the accounts were still active. Four took 30 days to de-activate. The remaining 18 were de-activated within 24 hours of the employee's termination."

Conclusion and/or Recommendations: "Our oversight system requires a comprehensive review."

Note that the *Introduction* begins with a statement of purpose, in the present (*analyzes*), not the past tense. This would normally be followed by some background information: who requested the review; who conducted it; when it took place. In a memo or letter report, *Introduction* should not be used as a heading.

Summary briefly presents the conclusions and recommendations of the report.

Findings could serve as a heading, but *Discussion* or *Analysis* are terms often used as the main heading for this section. Descriptive subheadings, appropriate to the subject, follow.

In an informal report, the *Conclusion* is not likely to be given a heading, especially if *Recommendations* follow in a numbered list. (See *Report* in Appendix A for a complete example.)

MINUTES

Minutes are essential to provide an accurate record of a meeting or discussion. Memories are unreliable and individuals can interpret information differently, so an objective distillation of the main points of discussion ensures that everyone present has the same information in the same phrasing. Inaccuracies or omissions are always addressed at the commencement of the next meeting, when these minutes are approved for the record.

The smaller the organization, the less likely that it will have a consistent, effective format for taking minutes.

A poorly organized, incomplete, and unclear record of what has been discussed and agreed to not only renders the meeting useless but can also lead to false conclusions and lasting disagreements.

The accuracy of the minutes depends on the alertness and accuracy of the minute-taker, who is generally a member of the group taking his or her turn at minute-taking.

Here are some tips for taking minutes:

1. Distribute a sign-in sheet so that you will have an accurate record of the attendees and, in particular, names, titles, and workplace information of new members or visitors.
2. Follow the agenda and use its headings.

3. For recording purposes, use initials only to identify speakers.

4. In the completed minutes, use initials under "Action by."

5. Outline the introductions to each of the main points.

6. Number the main points of discussion under each of the main headings.

7. Use active verbs (e.g., provided, circulated, summarized — see page 105).

8. Follow the speaker's train of thought.

9. Constantly be alert to W5 (Who, What, Where, When, Why) + How.

10. Keep up with the discussion. Do not ask for information to be repeated until the end of the meeting.

11. Write up the minutes as soon as possible after the meeting.

Formats for minute-taking vary extensively, but the following is an example of one that is both adaptable and effective

Example

	Minutes of Meeting
Minutes No.:	Ref.:
Prepared by:	Date:
Meeting date:	Time:
Location:	Project:
Subject:	
Present:	
Distribution:	

MINUTES

Point No.	Description	Action by	Date
1.0			
1.1			
1.2			
2.0			
2.1			
2.2			
3.0			
3.1			
3.2			
3.3			
3.4			
4.0			

If there are any errors or omissions, please contact:
Terry-Lynn Charles, 416-111-1111 ext. 222
terrylynn@schoolislife.com

DOCUMENT DESIGN

Format is the most important aspect of document design, but the visual presentation of the text can serve to attract or discourage a reader. Use plenty of white space to open up the text and make it visually attractive.

Which of the following would you choose to read first?

Because purpose and content are situational, these ratios will vary. If you take a few minutes more to plan, you'll probably need a few minutes less to write. If you take longer to write, you might need a little less time to revise. No writing task is ever the same as the last one, but you must give fair attention to each stage of the process.

A young man once told me that he assigned 100 percent of his time to writing, with the explanation that since writing was the task, why waste time with planning and revising.

Though his view was extreme, most people do assign too little time to planning and revising.

They're anxious to get started. They're unsure how to plan, or they feel they don't have time to plan. They define revision as proofreading — a spell-check followed by a quick scan for obvious errors.

Because purpose and content are situational, these ratios will vary. If you take a few minutes more to plan, you'll probably need a few minutes less to write. If you take longer to write, you might need a little less time to revise. No writing task is ever the same as the last one, but you must give fair attention to each stage of the process. A young man once told me that he assigned 100 percent of his time to writing, with the explanation that since writing was the task, why waste time with planning and revising. Though his view was extreme, most people do assign too little time to planning and revising. They're anxious to get started. They're unsure how to plan, or they feel they don't have time to plan. They define revision as proofreading — a spell-check followed by a quick scan for obvious errors.

I once saw a brilliant, three-page interior design proposal presented in the latter format, and no one could read the document to the end. The designer, for all his artistic and conceptual talents, had presented his verbal descriptions as if they were bricks in a wall.

Creating generous margins and white space between paragraphs or main points is a simple and effective method of inviting your reader into your document. Notice how this very simple letter manages to draw attention to itself:

Spiritus Capital Inc.
260 Maple Wood Blvd.
Vancouver, B.C. VEJ 3K8
Canada

June 4, 2010

TO HOLDERS OF COMMON SHARES

You are invited to the Annual and Special Meeting of holders of Common Shares of Spiritus Inc. that will be held in the Grand Salon of the Harbourview Hotel, 1550 Ocean Blvd. East, Vancouver, British Columbia, on Wednesday, September 9, 2009, at 2:30 p.m.

The items of business to be considered at this meeting are listed in the Notice of Meeting and described more fully in the attached Proxy Circular.

Should you be unable to attend the meeting, it would be appreciated if you would complete, sign, and return the Proxy Form to our transfer agent, ShareTrust Company of Canada, in the enclosed envelope.

Yours truly,

David Levine
President and Chief Executive Officer

Now you're well prepared to begin crafting your message in the form of an outline, which completes the planning stage. Having reached the end of this chapter, you may be surprised at how much work is involved in planning a non-routine message. But it's actually not work, it's strategic thinking. It takes relatively little time to accomplish and ensures you know where you're headed and how best to communicate that to your reader. The information in the next chapter will show you how to get there.

OUTLINE YOUR MESSAGE

Most of us learned how to make an outline at some point in our schooling and then immediately forgot about it when we left school. In the rush to get things done, many business people neglect this vital planning step and take a hit-and-miss approach. As shown by the following testimonial, this can definitely keep you awake at night.

Lionel B.

Lionel was a young man on the move and already a Team Leader in Customer Accounts Administration. He wrote daily e-mails, weekly team evaluations, and monthly reports, as well as revising departmental policies and procedures. Affable and energetic, he came across as an organized, efficient employee with middle-management potential.

When I asked Lionel how he wanted to improve his writing, he told me that he wanted to increase his confidence. He showed me a two-page report that he had completed at work. It was well organized and contained only a few minor errors.

"How long did it take you to write this?" I asked.

"About two hours," he replied. "But sometimes I can finish this kind of thing in less than an hour."

"Depending on how complex it is?" I asked. Two hours was way too long for what he had shown me.

"At the same level of complexity," he said. "With some I'm really fast, but with others it takes much longer . . . too long."

"And you miss a deadline?"

Concern showed on his face. "Yes, sometimes I do miss a deadline."

"Do you have any idea why you're sometimes fast and sometimes slow?"

"Oh, sure," he said, his face brightening. "Sometimes I figure out what I'm trying to say almost as soon as I start writing, and then I just go with it. But other times I write and write and write, and I still don't know where I'm going with it."

"So you just begin to write about the subject and continue to write until you've figured out where you're headed with it?"

"Exactly," he said. "I discover what I want to say as I write."

"It doesn't sound like a very reliable method," I ventured.

"Not always. I usually have to work on it at home."

"Have you ever tried using an outline?" I asked.

He looked a little embarrassed. "Other people have mentioned that. The problem is I've never made an outline, so I just start writing and hope for the best."

My best advice to Lionel? *Outline beats deadline every time.*

Creating an outline involves pre-thinking about your message. If you leave all your thinking to the writing stage, you risk running out of time.

Another benefit of producing an outline is that it reduces the anxiety that comes with every new challenge. As illustrated in the following example, 1,200 ideas coming at you is paralyzing. But once you take charge and consider your purpose and your reader, this number will vanish and you will be able to focus on the four or five ideas that really count.

Philip D.

"One day my boss called me into his office and asked me to write a sales letter. He wanted to describe the company and sell its services to a much desired prospective client. Having no choice in the matter, I politely agreed, but back at my work station I broke into a cold sweat. My fear was not about what I would say in the letter, but rather how I would organize the 1,200 ideas that I had. What would be the best thought to write first? What should I end with?"

As you begin planning your message, you are already on firm ground:

- You know what you're trying to accomplish.
- You know what your reader is likely to need from you.
- You know the most appropriate format by which to communicate it.

The outline stage completes the triangle illustrating the interdependence of *purpose, audience,* and *message.*

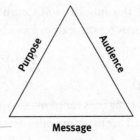

Message

Constructing an outline is just another form of problem-solving, requiring creativity, concentration, and determination. Once you've had sufficient practice, this process will take only a few minutes of your valuable time, and it will be a reliable guide to follow while writing your document.

CREATING AN OUTLINE

Let's say your supervisor has asked you and your colleagues to provide ideas on how to improve the quality of your team's sales presentations.

You create your outline in four distinct steps:

Step 1:
IDENTIFY THE MAIN ORGANIZING PATTERN

Overall, what is the relationship between your purpose and the general content of your message? Knowing this will help you select and organize specific points to achieve your goals.

Here are the most common ways of looking at the relationship between your purpose and the content of your message.

Informational

You may need to provide information — a meeting date, for example, or minutes. Or you might be writing a cover memo for more complex information that is being transmitted via attachment or mail. Your points are straightforward and no backup is required.

Persuasive

Because your goal is to convince the reader of something he/she will not consent to automatically, you need to carefully consider which points you will include and begin with your most persuasive.

Problem/Solution

Are you identifying a problem and proposing or requesting a solution? Are you outlining the solution to a previous problem? The details of each must be clearly separated and explained.

Problem/Solution can be combined with *Informational* or *Persuasive*.

Cause and Effect

In relation to a particular incident, are you examining the causes or the effects? You may be asked to explain why (the causes) you have gone over budget (the effect) or the benefits (effect) of offering more flexible work hours to boost the morale (cause) of your staff.

Comparison

When considering alternatives, detailed comparisons are often made. These comparisons can assist in choosing between products, procedures, or courses of action. They are frequently used in decision-making scenarios: what happens if we do

X, compared with Y? Comparative data are often displayed in a table. (See *Proposal* in Appendix A.)

Classification

Descriptions and analysis often involve an examination of *types*, which are subsections of a larger subject. If you worked in Human Resources, for example, you might be involved in revising or creating job descriptions, classifying them according to a hierarchy of responsibility and accountability.

Clearly, Problem/Solution applies to the scenario of providing ideas on how to improve the quality of your team's sales presentations. Weak presentations are the problem and your suggested improvements are the solution.

Step 2:
LIST AND SELECT YOUR MAIN POINTS

Start by reviewing your *Purpose* and *Audience.* What points do you need to include in your message that will achieve your purpose with this reader?

1. More training on PowerPoint.
2. Trying to say too much.
3. Better knowledge of customers' needs.

A novice writer might just write these points in full sentences and feel that the job is done. You know that more detail is required. Ask the questions *Who, What, Why, When, Where,* and *How* for each item on the list. The answers may also uncover some points you've missed:

1. **What** features?
2. **How** are the presentations too long or are they confusing?
3. **What** knowledge is lacking?
4. More time is required. **How** much? **Why? Where** will this time be found?

Note that No. 4 is an additional point. As you review your list, it occurs to you that if your team can achieve Nos. 1 to 3, there will be no need for No. 4, so you delete it from your list.

You will support each of your points with the following solutions:

1. Add zip; reduce word count.
2. Shorten length; leave future for follow-up; focus on immediate needs only.
3. Web site monitoring; questionnaire; follow-up.

Step 3:
SEQUENCE YOUR POINTS

You want to sequence your points in a way that makes the most impact on the reader. There are three ways of doing this, depending on the subject matter and your purpose.

Chronological Order

Use chronological order when the subject is time-based. For example, you may be describing a series of events that led to a conclusion or you may be providing a historical context. This order is also used for giving instructions, where you sequence the steps, first to last. Or if you are working on a long-term project, you will be expected to file progress reports, indicating where you are on your time line.

Order of Importance

Use this sequence when you feel some of your list items have priority over others, or when you need to persuade your reader to take a particular action. You simply rank your points, placing the strongest first.

How do you know which is your strongest point? By focusing on the detail that is likely to have the best chance of achieving your purpose. *If you were given the opportunity to make only one point, which would it be?*

Spatial Order

Though rarely applicable to business writing, this organizational pattern is very common in technical writing. For example, a photocopier technician would be able to describe how the parts are designed to function and what is causing them to malfunction. This sequence would enable you to picture how the key parts relate to one another.

In relation to the sales presentation scenario, after going over your list of three points, you decide that a more effective order is 3, 2, 1: customers' needs; saying too much; more PowerPoint training.

Why is this sequence more effective? You believe that increasing PowerPoint proficiency will be the easiest to achieve, while identifying customers' needs will be the most difficult. *Therefore you want to signal its importance by placing it first.* You reorder your supporting points accordingly.

Step 4:
FRAME YOUR MESSAGE

You now have three points, with suggestions for improvement. You decide to use a heading for each. You will use the generic organizational structure for an e-mail or short memo discussed in Tip Three:

1. Purpose or Main Point
2. Supporting Points and Detail
3. Close/Conclusion

Your outline looks like this:

— Input on Sales Presentations

— Three areas

1. **Better knowledge of customer's needs**

    - complete a questionnaire
    - post-meeting follow-up
    - monitor their web site

2. **Including too much**

    - limit to 30 minutes
    - focus on immediate needs only
    - address future needs in follow-up

3. **More training with the use
   of PowerPoint**

    - add zip
    - reduce word count
    - read less

Looking forward to the discussion.

(The completed e-mail is in Appendix A.)

How long has it taken you to get this far? Probably between 5 and 10 minutes, and your document is almost written.

Let's say you had 30 minutes set aside for this writing task. You want to leave at least five minutes for revision, so you give yourself 15 minutes to write up your outline. If you need less time for the outline, you will have more time for revision.

With practice you will incorporate these steps naturally, as with any skill that you have perfected.

Your points are now organized and structured, and you have a clear idea of what you want to achieve. You can now begin to write with the confidence that your document will be effective and that it will be delivered on time.

PART TWO
WRITE ACCORDING TO PLAN

With your planning completed, you can write with confidence, *according to plan*. Your outline consists of main points, in a logical order. For the actual writing, you will flesh out these points by applying techniques that answer the following questions:

*   Do you need an introduction?
*   What is the best evidence to support your points?
*   Should you use *I* or *We* or *They*?
*   How long should your sentences be?
*   How can you make the document *flow*?
*   How do you know if the grammar is correct?
*   How can you recognize unnecessary words?
*   How do you write a conclusion?
*   Where should recommendations go?

You should allot about 60 to 70 percent of your available time to writing this first draft.

The most important consideration in workplace writing is to get to the point quickly, support your point with persuasive detail, and state how you think the reader should use the information. Always aim for accuracy, simplicity, and clarity. Employees whose writing experience is mainly academic often discover that they haven't learned how to achieve these goals. For example, they may include a long description of the events leading up to their main point, which inevitably includes superfluous details that the reader must wade through before understanding the point. When finally they reach their main point, they may neglect to back it up with essential details or fail to connect their sentences in a logical manner. Overwriting by using too many words is another common weakness.

Because all these factors can be overwhelming, it is useful to visualize the basic materials that are used in all writing projects. You start with words, which are labels used to describe our exterior and interior worlds. You combine words into sentences that express one or more thoughts. Sentences are arranged logically into paragraphs that focus on a single idea. A series of paragraphs make up memos, letters, and reports. You used these same building blocks in writing essays, although you may not have been aware of it.

To these fundamental elements you apply techniques that create strong sentences, support and connect your points, and ensure that each word you use contributes to creating a document whose message is clear and complete.

William Strunk, the author of *Elements of Style*, famously put it this way:

> Vigorous writing is concise. A sentence should contain no unnecessary words, a paragraph no unnecessary sentences, for the same reason that a drawing should have no unnecessary lines and a machine no unnecessary parts. This requires not that the writer make all his sentences short, or that he avoid all detail and treat his subjects only in outline, but that every word tell.

This excellent advice requires that you take a disciplined approach to writing your document. You've worked hard to produce a good outline — don't squander that effort with lazy description, rambling sentences, or poorly connected ideas. It's easy to write much more than your reader needs. Be selective. Give your reader only what is essential. As you will learn in the next chapter, this disciplined process starts with the material you select to support your points.

SUPPORT YOUR POINTS

It's show time!

Vanessa P.
"When I need to write something it will take me forever to come up with two points and then I don't know what to say about them. I also tend to mix up my points, moving to another point before I have finished with the first point."

Terry D.
"I work in marketing where many decisions are made over e-mail. I am often asked to articulate the reasons I support or don't support upcoming projects. My arguments don't come across as concise or powerful insights."

When you wrote essays, you probably got most of your points through research and then struggled to put them into your own words.

With workplace writing, *your own words* are usually the only words you have, so you have to find a way to get them into your document or you won't have a document.

Identification of Purpose and Audience is the essential starting point. Asking W5+How for each of your points can also help to produce more details.

Vanessa doesn't appear to have a clear idea of either her purpose or her reader. She expects points to just pop into her head, and when they eventually do, she can't support them or sort them out because she hasn't got anything to relate them to.

Terry may have some trouble with analysis but what is most noticeable to his readers is that he is unable to provide sufficiently detailed feedback. In other words, he doesn't support his points in a convincing way. The details might be in his head, but they don't make it onto the page.

How much detail do you need? As much as required to satisfy your reader.

Providing detail can be as simple as offering the date of a meeting (you might want to add the detail that coffee and tea will be available), or confirming your attendance, or reporting the acceptance of a proposal.

However, if you want to make a case for renewing the lease on your office space, in spite of a hefty rent increase, you will need to include *two, three, or four* detailed reasons. It isn't sufficient to say "This is a good location," or "The staff is comfortable here." On the other hand, there is no point in creating a long list of points that includes minor details that are already known or can be assumed.

Use the following kinds of detail to support your main points:

DESCRIPTIVE DETAILS

Descriptive details are useful if, for example, you are describing the kind of office space your staff requires or the proposed outcomes of a new advertising campaign or marketing plan. The suggestions for improving sales presentations, shown in the previous chapter, consist of descriptive details.

EXAMPLE 1

Subject: Office Space Update

Main Point: We've incorporated your suggestion to locate marketing and sales on the same floor. The architects have promised new drawings by the end of next week.

Supporting Details: Briefly, the changes are as follows:

- Square footage increases from 7,500 sq. ft. to 12,500.
- Work stations increase from 25 to 40.
- Reception will be shared.

- Executive offices increase from two to four, with south-facing windows.
- IT service will be shared.
- Stationery supplies will remain separate.
- Coffee room will be expanded to 500 sq. ft.

(Note most important to least important sequence.)

EXAMPLE 2
Subject: Taste of Technology

Main Point: Thank you for agreeing to participate on the Planning Committee for the Taste of Technology event, scheduled to begin in early September.

Background: As you know, women account for only 9 percent of undergraduate enrolment and 5 percent of graduate enrolment in science and engineering programs in universities and colleges.

Supporting Details: The Taste of Technology campaign will give high school girls the opportunity to tour companies involved in the fields of medical and pharmaceutical science, information technology, and civil engineering. The tours will last a full day and will be repeated at three-month intervals so that each student can visit all three areas during the school year. At each site the students will be given the opportunity to assemble a simple piece of technology, such as an electronic circuit. Following each visit, students will be expected to complete a short essay describing what they learned. These essays will substitute for the missed class time.

(Note the use of chronological sequence.)

FACTS

Sergeant Joe Friday, the detective in the old TV series *Dragnet*, quickly tired when witnesses provided too many irrelevant details. His exasperated reminder, "All we want are the facts, ma'am," became the signature phrase of the series.

By definition, facts are real, not imagined or inferred. If in doubt, leave them out.

You would use facts in a performance review (backed up by examples and descriptive details); you might refer to factual guidelines found in professional standards, such as Generally Accepted Accounting Principles; you would state the facts when reporting an incident or the results of an action. You would also use facts to make a case for renewing your office space, in spite of a hefty rent increase. In the following example, the informal tone indicates that the writer and the reader enjoy a close collegial relationship.

EXAMPLE

Subject: Recommendation for Lease Renewal

Main Point: There are several very good reasons why we should renew the lease on our premises.

Supporting Details: The most important reason is that we're near public transit, and commuting delays are rare. Second, we worked hard to get the layout we wanted, and it would be a shame to start over. Third, the building is well maintained and our concerns are addressed immediately. Fourth, anything comparable and cheaper would be miles from here, and the cost to morale would not be worth the savings.

(The supporting details could also have been presented as a numbered vertical list.)

NUMERICAL DATA

In popular usage, numerical data are often referred to as *statistics*, but usually they're just numbers signifying dimensions, sums, and ratios. They deserve to be called statistics only when they are collected in vast groupings and analyzed for trends or patterns.

Numerical data are provable and, if accurate, provide specific, believable detail not available by other means. Words like "large" and "many" do not belong in workplace communication, because they are vague and open to interpretation.

EXAMPLE

Subject: Sales Order Backlog

Main Point: The sales order backlog for the company as of January 31, 2009, was $4.1 million versus $5.3 million at January 31, 2008.

Supporting Details: The backlog included $1.9 million in the Electronic Switch segment, compared with $1.3 million on January 31, 2008. This increase is due mainly to supplier delays caused by the earthquake in China in May 2008. The backlog for the Wireless Router segment was $2.2 million, a decrease of $0.3 million over 2008.

EXAMPLES

Examples illustrate the point you are making by providing snapshots that broaden your reader's understanding, or by showing its applicability in similar (and familiar) situations. You might also use examples to suggest theoretical outcomes:

- They took some radical steps to change their work culture. For example, they issued laptops to everyone and eliminated a dress code.
- A good example of an early paradigm shift was the Japanese automakers' concept of

organizing line workers into teams, with direct input into decision-making.

- Not every merger is a success story. For example, when Oakwood merged with Appleby, they continued to exist as parallel universes, often acting as though each were unaware of the other's existence.

- Although electronic books have many advantages over paper books, it appears that they have an image problem with the reading public. For example, reader surveys indicate that the e-book shell itself acts as a barrier that inhibits enjoyment of the text.

- The effects of such a severe downturn are difficult to predict and might, for example, lead to at least one bank failure.

- For example, let us assume that the North American auto industry fully recovers. Does it still make sense to offer thirty different models on six different body frames?

EXAMPLE

Subject: User Access to Applications

Main Point: We do not have an established procedure for notifying the IT department when internal user access needs to be modified or terminated.

Supporting Details: During our review we discovered the following examples:

- Eighty-four user accounts were missing from the Master list.
- The account of a terminated employee was active for three months.
- In 4 out of 20 cases requests for employee account modifications took 30 days to activate.

Aren't these also facts? Yes, they are. But they are being used to illustrate a problem that is caused *by the central fact*: the lack of an established procedure.

QUOTATION

Occasionally you may want to include a quotation that supports your point. You could also choose to paraphrase it, thus avoiding a direct quotation.

- Warren Buffett has said, "It's far better to buy a wonderful company at a fair price than a fair company at a wonderful price."
- According to Warren Buffet, it is better to pay fair value for a solid company than a bargain price for a mediocre company.

TABLES AND GRAPHS

Visual support can be very persuasive. When well-formulated and attractively presented, its impact is immediate. Because e-mail does not happily support graphics, it is best to restrict the use of tables and graphs to PDF and word-processing files or their printed versions. (See Proposal in Appendix A for an example of a table.)

Now you have all the information you require to begin writing your draft.

TIP SIX
WRITE STRONG SENTENCES

- When is a sentence too long?
- How do I get variety in my sentences?
- What's the difference between active and passive voice?

Strong sentences convey your message with impact and authority. Weak sentences distract your reader and sabotage your message. Sentences are the main building blocks of your text, and their meaning has to be clear on first reading. Your goal is to write every sentence with clarity and precision. As with any skill, this can be accomplished with knowledge and the application of certain techniques.

BASIC ELEMENTS

SUBJECT
Who or what is controlling the action of the sentence? It could be a person (I, you, he, she, we, they) or a thing (the company, the government).

The subject gives a voice to the sentence. In a novel, that voice might belong to a character with a Texas accent and certain oddities of speech. In workplace writing, that voice is always your voice, speaking either for yourself or for the organization that you represent.

VERB

The verb describes the action being taken by the subject of the sentence, placing it in the present, the past, or the future.

OBJECT

The object is the target of the action.

ACTIVE VOICE

When the subject (S) controls the action, it precedes the verb (V), and the object (O) follows the verb:

We (S) dropped (V) the ball (O).

A sentence with the sequence SVO is an active sentence, or *a sentence in the active voice.*

PASSIVE VOICE

Here the sentence pattern is the reverse of active — OV(S) — with the subject now an agent of the action and usually only implied:

The ball was dropped (by someone).

The passive voice should never be used in direct workplace communication because it doesn't assign responsibility for the action taken.

A second reason to avoid the passive voice is that the subject and the verb are the two most important elements of a sentence. *The passive voice obliterates the subject, leaving only the verb, which will rob your sentence of its vitality.*

The passive voice is best suited to technical description, where the subject is both impersonal and repetitive.

Example

A *newspaper description* of the pre-launch of the Space Shuttle would read like this:

> Engineers seal the capsule four hours before the countdown is scheduled to begin. They electronically activate the four hatch clamps and connect the exterior oxygen supply to a self-sealing pressure coupler. They maintain radio contact through the standby communications port, which is automatically disconnected at lift-off.

A *technical description* would read like this:

The capsule is sealed four hours before the countdown is scheduled to begin. The four hatch clamps are activated, and the exterior oxygen supply is connected to a self-sealing pressure coupler. Radio contact is maintained through the standby communications port, which is automatically disconnected at lift-off.

SENTENCE STRUCTURE

Always convey your information in digestible amounts.

At least 50 percent of the sentences in workplace documents contain only one main thought; no sentence should be more than 30 words long, unless it is contains information displayed as a vertical list.

EXPRESSING ONE MAIN THOUGHT

A sentence expresses a complete thought. All you need to express a complete thought are a subject and a verb:

Profit has declined.

This sentence is not very useful, because it contains so little information. Your reader will have questions:

- What is the overall profit?
- Did the profit decline in one division?
- Does this statement refer to quarterly or annual profit?
- How much has profit declined?
- Why?

With each sentence you write, always be clear about what you want to communicate. Check by asking yourself *who, what, why, where, when,* and *how*:

Company profit declined to 3 percent this quarter, due to lower sales.

Now the sentence contains specific information. You might be tempted to compare this performance with that of previous quarters:

Company profit was 5 percent in the first quarter, 4.8 percent in the second quarter, and 4.4 percent in the third quarter but declined to 3 percent this quarter, due to lower sales.

This sentence contains too much information between the subject and the second verb. Instead, include the information in two sentences:

Due to lower sales, company profit declined to 3 percent this quarter. This is a significant reduction from 5 percent in the first quarter, 4.8 percent in the second quarter, and 4.4 percent in the third quarter.

In the following passage, all sentences but the last contain a single thought:

The company's legal position requires clarification. It may be that you are liable for the full amount of the loan. Therefore a contingent liability exists and should be properly accounted for. One way to do this is to estimate the amount of loss. A review of the loan status and financial position of Westdale Bathroom Accessories is required. An accrual should then be set up, and a full note disclosure should be included in the financial statement.

The simplicity and directness of single-thought sentences are highly desirable in workplace communication, but if you overdo it your reader will beg you to get moving and make the obvious connections.

Example

There are multiple tests performed on all geosynthetics. Tests measure tensile strength and permeability. Tests also measure how much pressure it would take to puncture a geotextile. Mullen burst tests are performed on geotextiles. This test measures the amount of force it would take to puncture a geotextile. It is measured in MPA. A machine gradually applies pressure to a needle until the needle goes through the geotextile. The force needed to do so is recorded.

This passage can be restated in two sentences:

Geosynthetics are tested for tensile strength and permeability. The Mullen burst test measures puncture resistance by recording MPA needle force required to penetrate the material.

COMBINING THOUGHTS

As the geosynthetics example illustrates, if all your sentences contained only one main thought, it would be difficult to indicate the relationships between them. Your readers need to be clear about these relationships, because if you leave them guessing, your meaning will be open to different interpretations.

If your meaning is open to interpretation, you have failed to communicate clearly.

For example:
Many patients dislike hospital food. The menus are prepared by nutritionists.

Does this statement suggest that nutritionists prepare tasteless food?

The company is buying back its own shares. Their stock price has fallen sharply.

Is the buyback causing the share value to drop?

A second good reason to combine single-thought sentences is to include sentences of greater length and complexity. Sentence variety makes your writing more interesting and therefore more effective.

There are two basic structures for combining thoughts in a sentence:

1. Connect with Coordinating Conjunctions
There are six coordinating conjunctions: *and, but, or, nor, so, yet.*

For is sometimes included as a seventh, but it is rarely used as a conjunction in North American English.

These conjunctions can also be used to join single words: *pencils **and** paper; painful **yet** necessary.*

When these conjunctions are used to connect two or more thoughts, remember that *each thought must contain a subject and a verb:*

Margins (S) have been (V) lower this year, *but* we (S) predict (V) they will increase by 2 percent next year.

Either we (S) reduce (V) capital costs, *or* we (S) reduce (V) our workforce.

Social assistance budgets (S) have been cut back (V), *so* more people (S) are living (V) on the streets.

Notice that in these sentences a comma always precedes the conjunction. This ensures that the reader recognizes the two parts of the sentence.

You can also substitute a semi-colon for the conjunction:

Margins have been lower this year; we predict they will increase by 2 percent next year.

Semi-colons are not commonly used in workplace writing, however, because the precise relationship between the two sentences is left unstated.

2. Connect with Subordinating Conjunctions

Here is a list of the most commonly used subordinating conjunctions:

After, although, as, because, before, even though, even if, if, since, that, unless, until, when, where, which, while, who, whose

Subordinating conjunctions allow you to indicate a broad range of relationships:

Although many patients dislike hospital food, the menus are prepared by nutritionists.

The company is buying back its own shares, *because* its stock price has fallen sharply.

The Bank of Canada, *which* normally plays a monitoring role, has acted aggressively to lower its interest rate.

This is the same problem *that* caused us so much concern at this time last year.

Their art director, *who* some believe is the best in the field, accepted the award on behalf of the entire team.

By using both coordinating conjunctions and subordinating conjunctions, you can present the same content in several ways:

Although the price of fuel has gone down, many airlines are still adding a surcharge.

Many airlines are still adding a surcharge, *even though* the price of fuel has gone down.

The price of fuel has gone down, *but* many airlines are still adding a surcharge.

The price of fuel has gone down. *However,* many airlines are still adding a surcharge.

In spite of the lower price of fuel, many airlines are still adding a surcharge.

Many airlines are still adding a surcharge, *in spite of* the lower cost of fuel.

Dos and Don'ts

1. Do not run two sentences together without connecting them:

Social assistance budgets have been cut *back more* people are living on the streets.

2. If a sentence contains a subordinate conjunction, do not separate the two parts with a period, because this will result in a sentence fragment. You can always spot a sentence fragment, because the sentence makes no sense:

Although many patients dislike hospital food. The menus are prepared by nutritionists.

3. When you begin with a subordinate conjunction, a comma is placed before the subject of the next thought. This ensures that the reader recognizes the two parts of the sentence.

Although the price of fuel has gone down, many airlines are still adding a surcharge.

A document with a simple message will probably contain mostly short sentences whose relationship is obvious. A document with a more complex message will contain a variety of sentence structures, because the relationship between the numerous main points must be clearly indicated.

If you're worried that your sentence is too long or complicated, here's a simple test of its clarity: can you read the sentence out loud with a sense of complete authority over its contents? Or does it interrupt your train of thought and cause confusion in places? If it does, choose a different conjunction, or break your thoughts into two sentences.

SENTENCE TIPS

You may be full of enthusiasm for what you are writing, but that may not come across in your document. There are several reliable techniques for energizing your sentences:

1. USE ACTIVE VERBS

Verbs like *examine, analyze, investigate, cause, evaluate,* and *recommend* describe specific actions in precise terms. Compare these verbs with the following:

> This report *covers* [analyzes] methods used for storm water management.

> There *is* an investigation taking place. [We are investigating.]

> Shear force damage always *happens* when concrete structures come under lateral stress. [Lateral stress causes shear force damage in concrete structures.]

Here's a partial list of active verbs:

analyze	discover	plan
assess	document	prove
calculate	evaluate	recognize
compare	examine	recommend
conclude	execute	review
conduct	identify	solve
create	interpret	study
define	investigate	summarize
design	modify	survey
develop	observe	test
diagnose	operate	validate

2. USE A PRECISE VERB, NOT ITS NOUN FORM AND AN IMPRECISE VERB

Not: Buildings have *undergone an increase* in their energy efficiency.

But: Buildings have *increased* their energy efficiency.

Not: Our Quality Control department is *conducting an investigation* of your complaint.

But: Our Quality Control department is *investigating* your complaint.

Note that using the verb alone reduces the number of words required to make the point.

3. PLACE IMPORTANT INFORMATION AT THE END OF THE SENTENCE

> **Not:** You don't explain why in your analysis.
> **But:** Your analysis doesn't explain why.

> **Not:** We are committed to providing the highest level of service to each member of the business community, and your business is important to us.
> **But:** Your business is important to us, and we are committed to providing the highest level of service to each member of the business community.

4. DO NOT BEGIN WITH –ING OR –ED VERBS

> **Not:** Faced with substantial competition, we must ...
> Facing substantial competition, we must ...
> **But:** We are faced with substantial competition, and therefore we must ...

> **Not:** Having expanded our market share through acquisitions, we must now reduce our exposure.
> **But:** We expanded our market share through acquisitions, and now we must reduce our exposure.

5. KEEP SUBJECTS AND VERBS CLOSE TOGETHER

Not: The Rosewood Foundation (S), which began in 1985 and provides much-needed opportunities to teenage girls, including Camp Birchbark, located on Lake Cambrian, is kicking off (V) its annual fundraising campaign on Saturday, March 1.

But: The Rosewood Foundation (S) is kicking off (V) its annual fundraising campaign on Saturday, March 1. For 25 years the foundation has provided much-needed opportunities to teenage girls, including Camp Birchbark, located on Lake Cambrian.

6. AVOID VAGUE REFERENCES

We paid too high a price for office space in Lakeview Towers, and we should take steps to ensure that this doesn't happen in the future.

Q: What does *this* refer to? Paying too high a price or using Lakeview Towers? Both?

Attendance in Phoenix was down this year, and some of the exhibitors are saying they may not participate next year. *It* may change by then, however.

Q: What does *it* refer to? The decision not to
attend? Economic conditions?

7. GIVE IMPACT BY CORRECTLY USING HOWEVER AND THEREFORE

However and *but* have the same meaning, but *however* is much more emphatic and requires stronger punctuation:

> Our Digital Imaging division is meeting expectations, *but* the Laser Truss Design division has fallen with the decline in housing starts.

> Our Digital Imaging division is meeting expectations; *however*, the Laser Truss Design division has fallen with the decline in housing starts.

> Our Digital Imaging division is meeting expectations. *However*, the Laser Truss Design division has fallen with the decline in housing starts.

The full impact of *however* is realized in the last example.

This usage also applies to *so* and *therefore*:

Profit in the Laser Truss Design division has fallen with the decline in housing starts, *so* we are monitoring that situation closely.

Profit in the Laser Truss Design division has fallen with the decline in housing starts. *Therefore,* we are monitoring that situation closely.
OR
Profit in the Laser Truss Design division has fallen with the decline in housing starts, *and therefore* we are monitoring that situation closely.

(See Tip Eight for more related sentence tips.)

SELF-TEST 1
Revise the italicized areas. (Answers are on page 203.)

1. If a window in the shape of a rectangle capped by a semi-circle has a perimeter of 24 feet. *What* dimensions should the architect choose for each in order to admit the greatest amount of light?
2. The market for hand-painted wood figurines is strong, *therefore* we are hiring more staff.
3. To meet demand, 14 new *staff have been* hired and we have enlarged the plant.

4. *There are* three companies who have met the tender deadline.
5. *A consultant has been hired* to improve our public relations.
6. I also had *clearance to handle classified information* in my position with Galileo Aerospace.
7. The marketing department, *which designs our communication strategy, including logo, signage, and media relations,* has been relocated to the east wing in order to be closer to the Senior Management team.
8. We were planning to complete the audit by the end of the week, *however* we have not been able to obtain all the necessary information.
9. *Deriving* most of our revenue from subscriptions, we are aggressively seeking to expand this base.
10. In 2008 the financial industry in North America lost a total of $1.2 trillion. *It* may take years to recover from *this.*

It takes a lot of practice to feel confident that you have written a sentence the best way you possibly can. There are so many ways to write it! With practice, however, you will begin to favour certain constructions and feel completely confident using them. These will become the essential tools in your communication tool box. As you build your confidence and refine your style, you will add new tools that will enable you to do an even better job. One of these is the use of transitional words and phrases to connect your sentences, the focus of the next chapter.

CONNECT YOUR POINTS

Marisa D.
"I normally have a lot of trouble making paragraphs flow and finding the way each one supports the main idea. I feel inadequate at work when I see material that people have written in a very succinct way. When I analyze those writings it seems like you could not take out one word because everything matters and every word has a very specific function."

You design an outline, you fill in the details for your support, and you write your sentences — and when you read the text it doesn't sound quite the way you expected it to. The parts seem to be out of synch with one another. Noticing this deficiency in her writing, Marisa perceives that other people's sentences are linked by key words that do their job perfectly. She seems to suggest that this is a skill she does not possess. Yet these words, which are the main method for linking sentences and paragraphs, are available to everyone.

FLOW

One of the most common reactions people have when they read something they like is "The text really flowed." They sense a smooth, harmonious, uninterrupted movement from beginning to end.

In a well-written document the reader is taken along on the flow of the writer's thoughts, which seem to advance naturally along a well-marked route.

A sentence contains one or more thoughts. When you organize and connect a number of thoughts in a logical way, you are building a paragraph. A paragraph focuses on one main point or idea. An indent or space between paragraphs emphasizes their singular focus.

How is it that these thoughts and ideas seem to flow? And how is it that we so easily recognize when they don't?

Compare the following:

The program would provide assistance in several areas. Families with infant children require nurturing and nutritional support. Neighbours require supportive connections. Play opportunities are not adequate. Health, vision, speech, and language issues are a problem. School culture needs to be introduced within families. Our proposal is to work with children below grade one.

We propose to work with children below grade one. The program would provide assistance in several areas. The *most critical need* is for families with infant children to receive nurturing and nutritional support. *In addition,* infant play opportunities are not adequate, *and new facilities need to be made available. A second critical* issue that needs to be addressed is lack of access to medical facilities, *including those* for vision and hearing testing. *A third program goal* is the introduction of a schooling culture within families, *along with* more opportunity for language learning. *Finally,* neighbours require supportive connections *so that families do not live in isolation.*

The main goal of the two paragraphs above is to explain how a proposed program will help infant children, but only the second example adequately connects the thoughts.

The first example is a poorly organized list of problems the program would address. No goal is said to be more important than another, and no attempt has been made to guide the reader from one point to the next. We aren't even sure of the subject until we reach the last sentence.

The second example ties everything together, providing bridges and transitions from one sentence to the next in a clear, logical progression according to its order of importance. The passage also adds a few words of explanation to give greater meaning to some points.

Transitions highlight the connections between sentences and signal where the writer is heading. Transitional words and phrases also connect paragraphs, so that the entire document is stitched into a whole. The wording of the first and last sentences of each paragraph also contributes to the overall flow. The reader moves naturally from start to finish, because all the separate pieces flow together along a predetermined path.

TRANSITIONS

Transitional words and phrases are so obvious you may wonder why it is important to talk about them. The answer is simple: if you don't use enough transitions, or you don't use them wisely, your document will suffer. Inserting or replacing transitions is one of the most important functions of the revision stage.

As you saw in Tip Four, transitions help the reader understand your organizational structure and can have many functions:

TO SIGNAL CHRONOLOGICAL SEQUENCE
First, second, third (etc.); the first, the second, the third (etc.); then, next, last, finally;

after, subsequently; before, previously; rarely,
usually, generally, eventually, concurrently,
simultaneously, meanwhile (and many others,
of course)

These transitions connect the threads of a narrative:

In Vancouver we met with representatives of
Pacific Rim.... *Next,* we went to Seattle to meet
with Misty Coast.... *We followed this up* with a
meeting in Palm Springs with Aqua Desert....
Our *last* meeting was May 16, in Chicago, with
Paladin Group....

Without these simple time signals, the reader
might think that this was a random list in no particular order or possibly that it signalled order of
importance.

Depending on the amount of detail required,
this example could be written as one paragraph or
as separate paragraphs for each of the destinations.
The information could also be organized by date of
meeting.

Chronological transitional words and phrases
are also often used when describing the steps
required to complete an action. If the steps are
straightforward, they are usually itemized in a list
(see Lists, page 144). If they require explanation,

they are usually given a heading and displayed as a separate paragraph (see Chunking, page 142).

TO SIGNAL THE ORDER OF IMPORTANCE
the most important; another (important); also important (or, the least important); the first, the second, the third (in importance)

These words and phrases establish a priority sequence. Often, the most important point comes first:

The CEO of a public company has several critical responsibilities. The *most important* responsibility is to ensure shareholder profit. *Related to this* is the need to establish secure access to credit as required. *A third responsibility* is to expand market share for the company's products and services.

Our *most productive* meeting took place in Chicago, with Paladin Group. Discussions with Aqua Desert were *also productive*, but it will be several months before they can reach our production goals. Misty Coast and Pacific Rim are *unable to meet* our requirements.

TO SIGNAL SPATIAL ORDER

There is a huge number of prepositions and phrases that signal the physical placement of people and things. Here are a few of the less obvious ones:

> *Along the edge, straight ahead, at the top, at the bottom, surrounding, opposite, in the distance, beyond, within sight of, out of sight of, adjacent*

Precision is required in the use of these terms. Think of how difficult it is to give accurate travel directions or explain how to locate and use a software feature. In writing, these transitions are essential for orienting the reader to the spatial dimension and the reference points within it. Always start with the frame of the picture you are drawing and then fill it in, starting with the most dominant details:

> Modified-block letter style situates the sender's address and the complimentary close two spaces *to the right of centre*, giving a balanced appearance to the *top* and *bottom* of the page. The subject line is *centred* on the page. All else begins at the *left* margin.

A second category of transitions signals the relationship between two sentences, enabling you to show how your thoughts and ideas are connected to one another so the reader will not misinterpret your meaning. These connections also propel your thinking along a logical path to your conclusion.

TO SIGNAL AN ADDITION

And, in addition, also, too, as well as, in the same way, equally important, furthermore, one (reason), a second or another (reason)

These transitions indicate two related supporting points:

In addition to our efforts to develop new technologies ourselves, we may *also* seek partnerships with other companies. *Furthermore*, we may investigate the purchase of new technologies.

These transitions can also be used to link paragraphs that continue in the same direction:

In addition to the objectives outlined above, we believe that educational, medical, and community services should be housed in the same building.

In this example, you state that the preceding paragraph outlined one group of objectives, and now you are going to focus on a second group of objectives. It's a perfect bridge, or transition, between paragraphs. Here's another example of this bridging technique:

> We have targeted applications for our advanced imaging displays, the most attractive and popular electronic imaging screens in today's market. Most of our revenue comes from the sale of these screens, but a shift in market direction could reduce the demand for this product.
>
> Therefore, *in addition to our need to develop new technologies through our own research and development,* we must be prepared to consider the purchase of existing patents that would enhance our competitive position.

TO SIGNAL AN EXAMPLE

For example; for instance; such as; to illustrate

Note how these transitions are used with different sentence structures:

> *For example,* if market demand continues to shift to downloads, the DVD format will cease to exist.

If market demand continues to shift to downloads, *for example*, the DVD format will cease to exist.

You can choose any digitized reproduction, *for example* DVD format, and foresee its demise within a few years.

You can choose any digitized reproduction — DVD format, *for example* — and foresee its demise within a few years.

There are several risks from a downturn in business, *such as* loss of loyal customers, loss of key employees, and losses from downsizing.

They took risks *such as* expanding too quickly.

TO SIGNAL A COMPARISON
Similarly, likewise, similar to, in a similar way

Comparison enables you to show how one person, thing, or action is similar to another.

The fundraiser at the Park Plaza last week was successful largely because of the sponsorship by B&W Wines and the Lifford Wine Agency, who contributed the wines and the tasting notes. *Likewise*, the draw prize of a custom-designed wine cellar by Rosehill Wine Cellars drove total proceeds to a record level.

TO SIGNAL A CONTRAST

However, but, yet, although, nevertheless, in spite of, despite, in contrast, on the contrary, conversely, on one hand, on the other hand

Contrast enables you to show how one person, thing, or action is dissimilar to another.

Despite early technical difficulties that led many to doubt its adoption, the internet has changed the way we do business. *Nevertheless*, it is not suitable for every business model and many conversions have been costly failures.

The first sentence contrasts the early doubts with the eventual success. The second sentence contrasts the success with some eventual failures. The writer's thoughts are advanced in a connected and persuasive manner.

TO SIGNAL A CONCESSION

Although, even though, at least, still, of course, granted that, while it is true that

From time to time it will be in your best interests to concede a point. You want to be able to accomplish this action briefly and gracefully. When you grant a concession, you give up only one or two points, not the whole game.

> *Granted that / While it is true that* there were some design errors in the moulds, several other factors were responsible for the delays in production.

TO SIGNAL A CONCLUSION

> *Therefore, thus, so, consequently, as a result, finally, in summary, in conclusion*

As your train of thought unfolds, whether in a paragraph or an entire document, the reader begins to sense its progress toward a conclusion. Just as the logical connections between the sentences or paragraphs are signalled, so is the inevitable final statement or paragraph. The reader needs to sense this completion in order to be assured that you have achieved your purpose.

> In 2005 we sold our interest in sea-going navigational systems, and *as a result* we are no longer supporting further development of this technology.

Therefore, in light of the above concerns, we have decided to review the terms of this contract.

You can reach conclusions within paragraphs, at the end of paragraphs, and at the end of documents. The conclusion of a report or complex analysis is signalled by the heading *Conclusion* or *Conclusions*.

OPENING STATEMENTS

With any kind of document, your first need is to connect with your reader, and you don't want to waste time agonizing over the wording of that first sentence. Opening statements are difficult to write because they require a bridge to previous contact with the reader or a bridge to first contact.

There are numerous ways of making this connection:

- Thank you for your call today. I am confirming our meeting on August 22, at 3 p.m.
- I am the Assistant Superintendent of Plant Operations. Mr. Chua directed your inquiry to me.
- At our meeting last Tuesday you asked me to submit a report on three financial issues that

are of concern to Ironwood at this time. My analysis is provided below.

- As requested, we are pleased to forward our analysis and recommendations regarding the key financial issues facing Ironwood at this time: X, Y, and Z. The attached exhibits provide the relevant calculations.

CONCLUDING STATEMENTS

Concluding statements are easier to write because you have presented your information and are now thinking of the next step:

- As I have noted above, some issues require further discussion and I propose that we meet again early next week. Meanwhile, should you have any questions, please contact me at 111-1111.
- As you can see, both options have clear advantages, though "B" carries slightly higher risk. Please advise me of the Board's decision as soon as possible.
- If I do not receive your authorization by the due date, I will transfer the funds to your bank account.

RECOMMENDATIONS

If your purpose is to evaluate, or you are seeking a solution to a problem, you are likely to include recommendations based on your analysis and conclusion.

Recommendations are placed in a numbered list by order of importance. In a report, they are likely to be signalled by a heading that follows the conclusion (which will have its own heading). Some report styles highlight the recommendations at the beginning, right after the Executive Summary, or as part of it. For example:

Recommendations
As a result of this inquiry, the Board recommends that
1. the office of the CFO should take a more active role in the oversight of all budget holders;
2. all budgets should be reviewed monthly;
3. extraordinary expenditures should be red-flagged; and
4. budget holders should report shortfalls as soon as they occur.

If a recommendation concludes a memo or letter, it is introduced as follows:

Therefore, the Board recommends that the office of the CFO take a more active role in the oversight of all budget holders.

If multiple recommendations conclude a memo, they are presented in a numbered list:

The Board makes the following recommendations:

1. The office of the CFO should take a more active role in the oversight of all budget holders.
2. All budgets should be reviewed monthly.
3. Extraordinary expenditures should be red-flagged.

The presence of flow is essential for a document to be effective. Without it, your reader will sense your lack of authority and question your credibility. Flow happens when all your sentences are stitched together to form what the reader recognizes to be a coherent whole. Your reader will appreciate your efforts and will look forward to reading your next letter or report.

WRITE CLEARLY
AND EFFICIENTLY

Alexander G.

"I found what I thought was to be my dream
job in the fundraising office of a major research
hospital. They gave me six weeks to demonstrate that I could become an effective member
of the team. They said they would start me off
doing simple stuff, like writing thank-you letters and ensuring proper follow-up to donors.
Unfortunately, it took me forever to write my
thoughts in a clear and concise way, and when
my time was up they didn't offer me the job."

The first thing you need to be clear about in your
writing is basic grammar. For your reader, second-
guessing your grammar can become a fatal distraction. You also want to feel confident that you are
writing clear headings and formulating clear, integrated lists. And finally, you need to pay attention
to the easy-to-miss stuff that can interfere with the
reader's understanding — your word choice, your
phrasing, and the clarity of your thinking. It is clear

that Alexander's inability to do many of these things cost him a job he dearly wanted.

As you saw in Tip Five, the partnership between the subject and the verb controls the sentence, and their relationship must be respected.

SUBJECT-VERB AGREEMENT

If the subject is singular (I, you, he/she/it) the verb must be singular. If the subject is plural (we, you, they) the verb must be plural. This pattern is best illustrated by the present tense of the verbs *to be* and *to have*, because they are used not only for themselves, but also to create different forms for other verbs:

> I am, you are, he/she/it is; we are, you are, they are.
> I have, you have, he/she/it has; we have, you have, they have.

Dos and Don'ts

1. Notice the final "s" in "is" and "has." Do not confuse this "s" with a plural form. It partners with he/she/it, which are singular pronouns, and applies to all verbs in the present tense:

   - He works at IBM.
   - She flies to London once a month.

- It appears that inflation is under control.
- She isn't applying for the newly advertised position.
- It doesn't really matter which system we choose.

2. Sometimes the subject is difficult to identify:

> The cost of the renovations need to be amortized as a fixed asset expense.

The "s" in *renovations* may cause you to use a plural verb form, when in fact the subject is *cost* and the verb must be the singular form, *needs*.
Phrases that come between the subject and the verb ("of the renovation") do not influence their relationship.

3. Sometimes you forget what you started with:

> *The Mountain Pine beetle* has become a very serious problem in western Canada because *they* are killing trees.

> *The corporation* is gaining market share because *they* introduced new products.

In both cases, *they* should be *it*.

4. Subject-verb agreement with *either . . . or* and *not only . . . but also*:

> Not only several oil tankers but also a container ship was threatened.

The verb agrees with the subject closer to the verb. If this structure sounds awkward, you can always choose to rephrase the sentence:

> Several oil tankers and a container ship were threatened.

5. Pronouns that end in *-one, -body,* and *-thing*:

The verb that follows one of these pronouns is always singular:

> *Everybody* in the company *is* welcome to attend.
> *Everyone has* his/her opinion.

6. *Each, either, neither*:

These subjects are also always singular.

> *Neither* of those suggestions *is* a good one.
> *Neither* suggestion *is* a good one.

POINT OF VIEW

Through whose perspective do your thoughts unfold: through yours, through your company's, through the event that you may be describing? In every piece of writing, you must situate yourself in relation to your subject by establishing a *point of view*. Point of view has nothing to do with your opinion on your subject, but only with the lens through which you are viewing your subject.

First person singular (I)

Use *I* throughout your document if *your* observations or conclusions are of central importance.

Second person singular (you)

Use *you* throughout your document if you feel it is appropriate to address the reader. This is the point of view used in this book, because it is written as a guide. *You* is also used for written or spoken instructions, although it is usually only implied:

> [You] take the Parkway west and [you] turn south onto Briarwood Drive.

Third person singular (he/she/it)

This point of view is used when someone or something other than yourself or your reader is the subject. For example, you could be describing a circumstance, an applicable policy, or the actions of a third person.

> *The price of copper* was extremely high through-out 2008, but *it* fell significantly in the second half of 2009.

First person plural (we)

This point of view is used when you are representing your team, your department, or your company. In contrast to first person singular, here you include yourself as part of a larger entity that speaks with one voice.

Second person plural (you)

As you can see, the second person uses the same word for singular and plural. As the writer, you will know whether you are addressing one person or a group.

Third person plural (they)

Use this point of view when referring to a group or another company.

Dos and Don'ts

1. Avoid using the following:

   - I myself think
   - In my opinion

- In my judgement
- It is my belief
- Myself, I believe

2. Never refer to yourself as *the writer, this writer,* or *the undersigned.*

VERB TENSE

Tense is another word for *time.* Each verb tense signifies a particular time in which the action is taking place.

1. Use *going to* + the verb:

> We are *going to staff* several booths at Software Expo.

2. Use *will*:

> We *will staff* several booths at Software Expo.

PRESENT CONTINUOUS

The Present Continuous is different than Present Habitual tense because the action is or is implied to be occurring at the moment (now):

> We are taking steps to improve the situation.

That division is becoming too large.

We are proceeding too quickly with change.

PRESENT HABITUAL

The Present Habitual tense signifies a constant or repeated state or action in present time (every day, week, year):

The price of gold rises with the weakness of the US dollar.

Inventories are at an all-time low.

All public corporations file quarterly reports.

The difference between these two present tenses can be illustrated as follows:

Normally we work on Saturdays, but we are not working today because of a power outage.

SIMPLE PAST

The Simple Past tense is called *simple* because it is the most immediate (and least complicated) of the three past tenses in English. It signifies a completed action in the past:

We closed the office because of a power outage.

The company made record profits last year.

We lost the account last week but replaced it with a new one yesterday.

PRESENT PERFECT

Perfect is another word for *past*, so this tense combines present time with past time. It signifies an action that began in the past and *has continued* (this is an example of its use) into the present. In other words, the action is not completed. It is formed by combining the present tense of *have* with the *past participle* of the verb:

> This year we have been able to reduce losses in
> our retail division.
> We have completed your audit and will
> forward the results next week.
> They have operated at a loss since 2004.
> They have operated at a loss for five years.

PAST PERFECT

The Past Perfect tense signifies a past action that occurred *before* a simple past action. Since two past actions are being stated, the past perfect tense is necessary to distinguish it from the simple past action. It is formed by combining the past tense of *have* with the *past participle* of the verb:

> Mr. Newman's wife, Gladys, passed away last
> night. She *had been ill* for some time.

> Until we purchased Maritime Satellite
> Systems, our R&D *had been focused* on a global

positioning device that could operate under
water.

FUTURE

You can express the Future tense in three ways:

1. Use present continuous tense in a future
   context:
   We *are staffing* several booths at Software Expo.

2. Use *going to* + the verb:
   We are *going to staff* several booths at Software
   Expo.

3. Use *will*:
   We *will staff* several booths at Software Expo.

Dos and Don'ts

1. Be consistent:

   Just as you establish an overall point of view
   in a document, you also establish a dominant
   time that you must maintain. Are the events
   you are describing ongoing or are they complete? You can still choose to move back and
   forth in time, as long as you provide time signals that enable the reader to follow you.

2. Use present tense to introduce or present a report:

> The following discussion and analysis
> *provide* information that management
> *believes* is relevant to understanding
> certain decisions made in 2008.

The report has been written and is in the hands of the reader. Therefore, it would be inappropriate to say, "This report will provide. . . ." In the body of the report, however, you will choose the verb tense that suits the situation. This is usually the simple past tense, since you are reporting on events that have already occurred.

3. *Will* can imply certainty, and therefore commitment. Use the other forms of the future tense if it is not your intention to express certainty.

USING "IF"

"If" is a word that punches way above its weight, because it introduces three complex relationships that require unique sentence solutions:

1. "If" can introduce a real condition that has a possibility of being fulfilled:

If our final quarter's results *come* in as expected, we *will surpass* last year's record total revenue.

2. It can introduce an unreal condition that has very little or no possibility of being fulfilled and is therefore expressed in theoretical terms:

If our final quarter's results *came* in as expected, we *would surpass* last year's record total revenue.

3. It can introduce an unreal condition that was not fulfilled and was therefore expressed in theoretical (even wishful) terms:

If our final quarter's results *had come* in as expected, we *would have surpassed* last year's record total revenue.

If we *had been able to predict* the recent downturn, we *would have protected* more of our assets.

Dos and Don'ts

1. In example 2 the thought is expressed in present time, but the first verb is in simple past tense. This device essentially creates a time warp, signifying the unreality of the statement.

2. In example 3 the thought is expressed in simple past time, but the first verb is in past perfect tense. This signifies that the statement is two steps away from the reality.

3. Only the second clause contains *would*. It is never correct to use *would* in both clauses:

> If our final quarter's results *would come* [*came* is correct] in as expected, we *would surpass* last year's record total revenue.

PARALLELISM

Part of what makes flow attractive to the reader is the symmetry of sentences using repeated elements. If the flow of the sentence is interrupted by a word that doesn't fit the pattern of what came before, the reader is distracted from the meaning. Parallel structure is especially important when constructing lists.

NON-PARALLEL STRUCTURE

> Instituting *internal controls would provide* the capability of cross-checking, and *compliance* with Revenue Canada/Internal Revenue Service *would be ensured.*

PARALLEL STRUCTURE

Instituting *internal controls would provide* the capability of cross-checking and *would ensure compliance* with Revenue Canada/Internal Revenue Service.

CHUNKING

In workplace writing, information must be clearly written and presented so that its main parts and main points can be understood with minimum effort. *Chunking* is the technique of separating your message into logical blocks of information, often under a heading. Chunks could consist of an entire paragraph, or main points in a list. Spacing between chunks and the use of vertical lists are the visual evidence of chunking. To make the points as readable as possible, this book uses a lot of chunking.

HEADINGS

Like subject lines, headings need to be crisp and evocative. As you saw in Tip Four, often they function (*functional headings*) as part of the framework of a document — a report, for example. But you can choose to place your own *descriptive* headings within the body of a memo, a letter, or a report to highlight the different sections. Descriptive head-

WRITE CLEARLY AND EFFICIENTLY ◄ 143

ings should contain no more than four or five key words that capture the *focus* of the discussion or list that follows. First-level headings are usually bolded and often underlined as well.

INEFFECTIVE HEADINGS

- Recommendations for Sales Presentations
- Internal Control
- Admission Fees

EFFECTIVE HEADINGS

- Recommendations for *Improving* Sales Presentations
- Internal Control *Audit*
- Admission Fee Increase

Dos and Don'ts

1. Headings should begin with a noun, although sometimes the —ing form of the verb is appropriate. (Repaying a Loan; Calculating Interest)
2. Following a heading, do not announce your subject. The heading has already done that.
3. Do not use a heading if you have only a sentence or two of information related to the subject. Instead, include that information elsewhere.

4. Use title case (where the first letter of each content word is capitalized). See examples above.
5. For a subsection heading (a second-level heading), indent one tab. If your document has even more subsections, number each heading accordingly (1.0; 1.1; 1.1.1), but do not indent beyond the second-level tab.

VERTICAL LISTS

If you want to highlight three or more observations, reasons, facts, or findings, arranging them in a vertical list is the most effective way of presenting the information. Number the list if describing a procedure, a series of instructions, or a ranking, or if you want to refer to these items later in your text. There are three patterns:

First, the introductory statement is a complete sentence and each list item is also a full sentence:

Please consider the following recommendations:

1. Segregate the duties.
2. Replace two part-timers with a full-time position.
3. Bond the Head Cashier.
4. Implement surprise audits.

(*You should* is understood to preface each of these sentences.)

Second, the introductory statement is a complete sentence but each list item is not a full sentence:

The following changes would tighten your cash control:

- Segregating duties
- Replacing the two part-timers with a full-time employee
- Bonding the Head Cashier
- Implementing surprise audits

Third, the introductory statement is incomplete, and therefore the items in the list must complete the sentence:

You could tighten your cash control by

- segregating duties,
- replacing the two part-timers with a full-time employee,
- bonding the Head Cashier, and
- implementing surprise audits.

Dos and Don'ts

1. Note in the last example that each item ends with a comma, the second-last item ends with *and*, and the last item ends with a period.

2. Use a horizontal list for up to three items, or more if each item consists of only one or two words:

   Partners in Business offers professional development courses in resumé writing, sales presentations, and interviewing tips.

   The most important job-hunting skills are *(1) resumé writing, (2) sales presentations,* and *(3) interviewing techniques.*

3. Never place a colon after any form of the verb *to be* (is/are/was/were/will be):

   The most important job-hunting skills are: *(1) resumé writing, (2) sales presentations,* and *(3) interviewing techniques* [use of colon is incorrect].

4. Ensure that the list items are grammatically parallel.

SELF-TEST 2

Revise the italicized words and phrases. (Answers are on page 205.)

1. This report *will provide* information that management feels is relevant to recent decisions.

2. If our final quarter's results *would come* in as expected, we would surpass last year's record total revenue.

3. Half our business is generated in New Haven, and *Copenhagen generates the other half.*

4. The entire staff *is* concerned, but they are afraid to speak up.

5. *We have started* our business here in 2002.

6. The new sales manager is friendly, smart, and *shows a lot of enthusiasm.*

7. The three admin staff chosen *were*: Nika Rasky, Rami Faroud, and Emily Fong.

8. Neither of the two *are* suitable.

9. *It is my belief* that next year will show a positive return on investment.

10. The rising cost of raw materials *have* forced us to seek cheaper alternatives.

MAKE EVERY WORD COUNT

Don't use more words than necessary. Unnecessary words smother your message and place undue hardship on your reader. Why use 29 words when 10 can convey the message more clearly?

> We are experiencing an increase in the cost of photocopying. In an investigation of company procedures it was found that employees were not properly following the company photocopying policy. (29 words)

This is an example of a poorly constructed paragraph whose meaning is not immediately clear. Why write something in a way that you would never speak? The thoughts can be simplified into one clear sentence:

> Photocopying costs have increased because employees are not following policy. (10 words)

Another cause of word inflation is using bloated words and phrases like *completely eliminate* and *at the present time*. The local radio station announces "rain activity in the afternoon hours." Would you actually *say* that to someone? Do you tell people you were born "in the *month* of June"? Yet these undesirable spoilers frequently pop up in workplace writing. They are weeds choking your message, and you need to yank them out by the roots. (See *Grammar to Go*, page 99, for a list of unnecessary words and phrases.)

SIMPLIFY

The key to clear writing is to keep things simple. As soon as you overwrite, you will tend to repeat yourself or complicate the uncomplicated:

Another issue related to comfort is that of
    noise level.
Noise level also affects comfort.

Steel pipe does not bend very easily when
    compared to plastic pipe.
Steel pipe does not bend as easily as plastic
    pipe.

Places like China, Japan, and Germany have
    their own versions.
China, Japan, and Germany have their own
    versions.

SPECIFY
If you don't include specific details, your message
will be open to interpretation:

This year's staff picnic will be fabulous, with
tons of games and entertainment, great prizes,
and the best food ever.

Picnic day arrives and the employees can be
heard muttering, "I thought there would be shrimp";
"The prizes weren't all that great."

Dos and Don'ts

1. Avoid abstractions:

> This is a great product.
> That was the best move we could have
>   made.
> That was our strongest year on record.

What was *best* about the move? Even if the context clarified the meaning of these sentences, the words *great, best,* and *strongest* still contain no information. If, after a description of its benefits, you want to recommend a certain product, then say, *I recommend that we purchase X because it outperforms Y.*

2. Always quantify amount:

> Engineers pump the water from deep
>   down. (How deep?)
> We need to transfer a large sum of money.
>   (How large?)
> Just the right amount of binder is required
>   to harden the concrete. (What
>   amount?)

3. Don't introduce the detail with unnecessary description:

Engineers pump the water from very deep
down, not less than 1,000 m.
Engineers pump the water from a depth of
1,000 m.

This project will require a large sum of
money, at least $50,000.
This project will require at least $50,000.

The correct amount of binder, 20 percent
by volume, is required to harden the
concrete.
Binder, 20 percent by volume, is required
to harden the concrete.

Because it's so easy to forget to include essential details, you should note them in your outline. If
some don't occur to you until you are writing your
document, note them at the end of your document
file as you are writing and use them as required.

CLARIFY

You can keep a sentence simple and still not make
it clear. Oversimplification by the writer can lead to
bafflement in the reader:

As the person in charge of the project, I want to
bring this matter to your attention. (Who's in

charge? You, or the person you are writing to?)

Project A is 50 times larger than Project B. (By cost? By area?)

Although these designs are not yet practical, they are a good step forward in the renewable power industry. (To what part of the industry does that step belong?) Here's one possibility:

Although these designs are not yet practical, they are a good step forward *in the development* of the renewable power industry.

Always put yourself in the position of the reader. Have you included sufficient detail? Are your explanations clear?

VERIFY

Part of making every word count is ensuring that you have chosen the correct and most precise word. A spell-check program will not identify errors in the following sentences:

Out of respect for the memory of our founding president, we will observe a period of *morning*.

I would like to request a meeting at your *connivance*.

It's easy to be lazy and stick with the first word that comes to mind:

> **Not:** The checklist is for the inspectors to *check.*
>
> **But:** Inspectors *examine* (or *approve*) the checklist.

> **Not:** We have to change our *mentality.*
>
> **But:** Is *mentality* really the right word? Don't you mean *attitude*?

Dos and Don'ts

1. Don't use words to dazzle.
   New words and phrases appear every day. These are often buzz words, or words of the day. If you write *convergence*, are you using it because it's the most appropriate word, or because it sounds important? Resist using these words in your writing until they've stood the test of time (a couple of years, at least).

2. Don't use words you don't understand.
   If you misuse a word, you risk damaging your credibility. A senior vice-president of a bank, believing he has found a fresh word for *duplicate*, speaks of *duplicity* in all their key administrative systems. Oops. Check a dictionary to see how funny *that* is.

These risky words also include abbreviations and acronyms. If you can't write the full name, you haven't earned the right to use the short form.

3. Make sure you have the facts.

> *I believe* that accounting rules require estate trustees to invoice personal fees via a third party.

> Confirm your statements, and then you won't have to say *I believe*, and your reader won't have to say, *Are you sure?*

> It *seems* that in July half our staff is sick on Fridays.

> Find the actual percentage, and you can be sure of what you are saying.

4. When numbers are involved, make sure you do the math.

> A spokesperson for a safe-driver group quotes a statistic revealing that in 55 percent of the accidents involving teenage drivers, there was another teenager in the car. He concludes that if teenage drivers

were not permitted to carry teenage passengers, the accident rate would drop by close to 50 percent.

Has the spokesperson made a correct assumption?

5. Avoid stating the obvious.

We live in a time when our society depends on the movement of goods and people.

We are a large and complex organization.

In today's world, everything is happening faster than ever.

6. Avoid using outdated phrases.
Although you will encounter these dusty relics from time to time, in your own writing use the modern equivalents:

Avoid	Use
as per	as discussed
as per your request	as you requested
herein	(omit)

Avoid	Use
heretofore	(omit)
thereon, thereof, thereto	(omit)
this is to acknowledge	I have received/ thank you for
this is to inform you	(don't announce: omit)
pursuant to your inquiry	as you requested
enclosed please find	X is enclosed/I have enclosed X
attached please find	X is attached/I have attached X
earliest convenience	as soon as possible (or state time or date)
please be advised that	(omit)
you are hereby advised	(omit)
it has come to my attention	I have just learned that
it is our understanding that	we understand that

Avoid	Use
it is much appreciated	I appreciate
it is much appreciated if you	I would appreciate it if you
do not hesitate to contact me	please contact me
under separate cover	by courier, by post
the undersigned	(omit)

SELF-TEST 3

Revise the italicized words and phrases. (Answers are on page 206.)

1. The *cost of X is higher* than the cost of Y.
2. *Local print shops charge a higher price than our printing services if the print job can be performed in-house.*
3. *Due to the fact that* the shipment of servers has been delayed, unfortunately we will not be able to hold the training session *until some time in the near future.*
4. A consistent pattern of micromanagement tells employees that *they* don't trust their work or judgement.

5. *I would greatly appreciate it* if you would *give consideration to* the *eventuality of a combination* of the two departments.

When you apply the techniques discussed in Tips Six and Eight, both you and your readers will immediately notice improved clarity and impact in your writing. You will use fewer words, your sentences will be more powerful, and your layout will be crisp and attractive. You will also understand some important aspects of grammar, perhaps for the first time, which will give you greater confidence to express yourself beyond your self-imposed limits.

PART THREE

APPLY POLISH

If you have given yourself time for revision, you will enjoy the reward for all your painstaking planning and writing — the satisfaction of applying the finishing touches to something that you alone created. Whether a memo or letter or report, its organization and presentation say a lot about how much you value effective communication. Of course you want your readers to know that you are a conscientious, skilled communicator. You do not want to release a flawed document any more than you want to present yourself at a job interview wearing a wrinkled shirt.

Depending on the length and complexity of your document, the revision stage of the process may take one minute or several hours. Adding and subtracting content and vocabulary, rephrasing, and tightening, as well as cleaning up the mechanical errors that inevitably appear in first drafts, will ensure that your document has maximum impact on your readers. Within the limits of your available time, your goal is perfection. Readers will recognize the effort you have made to make your message clear, coherent, and concise. They will appreciate the accuracy of your spelling and grammar, the logical arrangement of your headings and paragraphs, your attention to detail — and they will look forward to receiving your next communication.

Tip Nine: Revise for Impact provides checklists for revision and explanations for some of the most commonly asked questions. Is it fair to expect you to correct something that you don't know is wrong? No, but it is fair to expect you not to repeat the error once it's been pointed out. As with any skill, if you want to become a better writer, you have to work at it.

Tip Ten: Write with Speed, Confidence, and Impact explains how you build confidence in your writing by applying the techniques that increase your planning and composition speed and that communicate your message with maximum effect on the reader.

REVISE FOR IMPACT

William S.

"I was working for a government department, and I was asked to send an all-government e-mail that contained an important announcement from the minister. Although I didn't write it, I made the mistake of not bothering to check for mistakes. Not only were there a lot of grammar and spelling mistakes, but the minister's name was misspelled! Because of this, I made not only myself look bad, but also my manager and the director of the department."

Irene W.

"Before I graduated, I used to have a few months to read books and analyze data, and report writing didn't seem to be very challenging. However, in my most recent job my new supervisor glanced at my first report for a few minutes and then told me she would rewrite it. I was embarrassed and asked if she could give me some feedback so I could resubmit it. My boss did provide some feedback, but because of time constraints she chose to rewrite the report herself."

Revision is the process of correcting and rephrasing. With a complex document that has given you trouble this can take a lot of time. But with documents of the length discussed in this book, revision can be accomplished in a matter of minutes. After all, your text is based on an outline that has a logical structure, your points are in order, and you have included the necessary details. Thus, you don't have to concern yourself with those aspects. Numerous examples of the revision process appear throughout this book.

The best way to revise is to read your work aloud. This forces you to read every word and hear every sentence.

CHECKLIST FOR CORRECTIONS

1. Is the format accurate in every detail?
2. Is the layout visually attractive?
3. When you spell-check your document, are you confident that you have the correct form of every word? If in doubt, verify with a dictionary.
4. Is your vocabulary accurate?
5. Does the sentence structure vary?
6. Is your grammar correct?

7. Have you followed the rules of basic punctuation?

CHECKLIST FOR PHRASING

1. Is your purpose clearly stated in the subject line or first sentence?
2. Are the language level and detail appropriate for your reader?
3. Have you used an appropriate tone of voice?
4. Do the connections between sentences and paragraphs make sense?
5. Does everything flow?
6. Are there any unnecessary words or phrases?
7. Is it clear what action you expect of your reader?

You don't have to put your document under a microscope, but you do need to test it with these questions. A first reading aloud will uncover most of the required corrections, and a second reading will suggest the need for some rephrasing. After that, let it go — and profit from your mistakes.

FREQUENTLY ASKED QUESTIONS

Here are the answers to common questions about grammar and punctuation. Knowing this information will help you to revise more efficiently and effectively. Over two hundred similar questions are answered in *Grammar to Go.*

> *When I'm writing a series of three or more words or phrases, do I place a comma before the final "and"?*
> The choice is yours. Most organizations use the comma, but some do not. Whichever approach you choose, be consistent.

> red, white, and blue
> or
> red, white and blue

> *How do I indicate possession when a singular word already ends in s?* Add **'s.**

Texas's oil industry; congress's plans; my boss's expectations

> *What is the difference between* it's *and* its*?*
> The first is a contraction of *it is* or *it has (been).* The second is the possessive form of *it: Its business has suffered.*

> *What is the difference between a dash and a hyphen?*
> The **em dash** (the length of the letter *m*) is a punctuation symbol used in a variety of ways to signal emphasis or interruption:

He held many foreign posts — in Singapore, Australia, Europe — but always called Chicago home.

We could take the acquisition route — but that's a discussion for another time.

The **en dash** (the length of *n*) indicates a span from start to finish:

1999–2002; 1–46

The **hyphen** connects two or more words so that they are read as one.

Some words are simply spelled this way: *two-thirds, self-paced*

Others are hyphenated only when used as modifiers: *part-time* employee, **but** they work *part time.*

An *up-to-date* chronology was presented. The chronology was *up to date.*

Does a period go inside or outside a quotation mark?

Periods and commas go inside a quotation mark.

One of the duties of the Compensation and Governance Committee is to "review

incentive bonus arrangements for senior
officers."

Can I start a sentence with and *or* but?
Not in workplace writing.

Is it correct to say less people?
No. Use *amount* and *less* for nouns, like *money*,
that don't normally have a plural form. Use
number and *fewer* for nouns, like *people* and
cars, that have a plural form. Sometimes *lower*
is the correct word: *lower earnings.*

What's the difference between affect *and* effect?
The first is a verb meaning *modify* and the second is a noun meaning *result.*

Inflation *affects* the economy, and one of
the *effects* is higher prices.

Do I say staff is *or* staff are?
If you know the members of staff, you are likely
to see them as individuals and therefore use
are. If they belong to another organization, or
if you are using the term in a general sense, you
are more likely to use *is.*

What's the best way to eliminate words?
Read the sentence and see what words you

can do without. In your anxiety to be clear, you may over-describe or over-explain, which places too many words in the way of clear comprehension. Make your sentences as lean as they can be, without cutting any of the essentials.

> In a natural environment there is a lot of grass and vegetation that helps filter rainwater into the ground.

First cut: In a natural environment grass and vegetation help filter rainwater.
Second cut: Grass and vegetation help filter rainwater.
Final cut: Vegetation helps filter rainwater.

Either the second or final version would work fine. You have reduced the original number of words from 19 to either 6 or 4, without losing meaning. Very impressive!

WRITE WITH SPEED, CONFIDENCE, AND IMPACT

John K.
"My biggest challenge is trying to go from essay writing (from my university days) to composing extremely efficient e-mail messages and letter reports."

My goal in the first nine chapters of this book has been to provide you with the techniques to meet this challenge, and my hope is that you will view the examples presented in Appendix A with a sense of mission accomplished. If you apply these writing techniques every time you write, soon you will experience a feeling of accomplishment, which in turn will give you the confidence to address any writing challenge and meet its deadline. Your ability to plan effectively will increase your speed, and your ability to write and revise with efficiency and clarity will give your document maximum impact.

With the exception of routine messages, every document presents a fresh set of challenges: a different purpose, a different reader, different content.

Without the skills to meet these challenges, in the past you likely saw them as insurmountable obstacles. Now that you possess the skills to meet these challenges, you can tackle them with the confidence that you will find a solution. As you accomplish your goals in one document after another, you will experience the unique satisfaction that comes from making meaning out of chaos.

SPEED

By *speed* I do not mean to imply a race to the finish line. In fact, that is something you want to avoid, because it means you have given yourself too little time to produce a competent result. Rather, I mean that by following a series of efficient steps you will save time by not wasting any of it. Undoubtedly, you have had the experience of trying to write something without sufficiently selecting and organizing the relevant information. This wastes time in two ways: either you procrastinate, making false start after false start, or you dash off with no clear direction, only to run out of road.

Efficient planning involves articulating both your purpose and the specific needs of your reader, then selecting and organizing the information that will achieve your goals. Selection of appropriate format also involves efficient decision-making. You certainly don't want to be in the final stage of writing a letter when you decide that you are actually writing a proposal.

Applying the steps outlined in Part One, "Think Before You Write," may consume 20 percent of your available time, but it will prevent you from wasting up to 80 percent of the rest of it.

Your writing speed will also increase by the application of the techniques for supporting and connecting your points — for example, by asking W5 + How to ensure that you have included all the pertinent information. Choosing the appropriate connecting words is another time-saver, because they clarify what you are trying to achieve in each sentence.

The ability to meet deadlines consistently is the result of careful planning, thoughtful writing, and disciplined revision.

CONFIDENCE

It should be clear that knowledge of technique and ability, refined through practice, will increase your confidence in every aspect of writing. In the Introduction to this book, I summed it up this way: *speed will allow you to meet deadlines, and impact will ensure that your document is effective. Call it the circle of confidence: you need confidence to succeed, and every success increases confidence.* With every success, you edge ever closer to mastering your organization's communication requirements. As your above-average writing ability is noticed, you will be asked to accept more complex challenges. Because large organizations place a high value on securing effective communicators, a promotion and higher salary are likely to follow.

IMPACT

Readers often use the same images to describe a document that has no impact: "It's flat"; "There's no life in it"; "It just lies on the page." What's missing? Energy, clearly. Emphasis. Detail. Connectedness. This kind of lifeless writing lacks assertiveness and conviction, and it's easy to assume that these same qualities are lacking in the writer.

All the techniques presented in Parts Two and Three contribute to creating impact in your documents. Impact is achieved by the use of precise details. Impact is achieved by word choice: a precise term versus a vague term; an active verb, such as "investigate," versus a limp version, such as "look into." Impact is also achieved by the use of a variety of sentence types and the connecting words and phrases that link them — a document that doesn't hang together can't have impact. A logical sequence of thoughts and ideas is also essential; without it, there is only disorder and confusion. Sound grammar creates impact; poor grammar creates nothing but distraction. Layout creates impact by presenting reader-friendly page design and by displaying vital information in well-constructed lists.

In the writing stage, you create impact when you choose precise words, create concise headings, and write clear sentences that flow logically from one to the next. In the revision stage, you create impact when you tighten loose connections, delete unnecessary words, and ensure 100 percent accuracy in content, language use, and layout.

Tips One through Ten describe the writing process from start to finish, with the ultimate goal of empowering you to incorporate all the tips into all your workplace writing tasks, whether they be short or long, simple or complex. When you have become practised at incorporating the tips, you will recognize that you are writing with speed, confidence, and impact.

Appendix A features polished examples of the six most common types of business correspondence: e-mail, memo, letter, short proposal, short report, and minutes. These represent your final objective. In each case the techniques involved in pre-writing, writing, and re-writing have been applied. No doubt you will come across modified versions of these types of correspondence, as well as formats not included here, such as those for sales letters and briefings. These models will be recommended by colleagues whose judgement you trust. Keep a copy of each on file and incorporate their best features into your own work. Writing is a dynamic process, and throughout your career you can continue to increase your knowledge and skill level with every document you read and every document you write.

APPENDIX A

EXAMPLES OF BUSINESS CORRESPONDENCE

The following pages present an example of a complete document for each of the formats discussed in Tip Three, followed by an analysis of the planning, writing, and revision techniques involved. You may choose to read all these examples or only those that apply to your own current writing needs. The scenarios simulate typical workplace situations that require written communication. Imagine yourself in these situations and, as you read the example that follows, test your knowledge of the techniques used. If you find yourself flipping back to some of the earlier chapters to refresh your memory, that is good news. It indicates that you want to do the best job possible. When you compare your analysis with the one I have provided, no doubt you will discover numerous similarities — and you may also have some valid suggestions of your own.

As your workplace writing improves by the repeated study and use of these techniques, you will begin to notice that they are used by other good writers as well. Some of their documents will impress you. Study them. What makes them impressive?

What can you learn from them? Use these opportunities to become an even better writer than you are right now.

E-MAIL
The following example is based on the outline, shown on page 77, that was created in Tip Four.

Scenario
Your supervisor has asked you and your colleagues to provide ideas on how to improve the quality of the team's sales presentations.

Example

Subject: Input on Sales Presentations

Here are my suggestions for improvement, with some ideas for how to achieve them:

1. Increase Our Knowledge of Customers' Needs
   - Monitor client web sites.
   - Get feedback via a questionnaire to help us plan the presentations.
   - Offer follow-up client consultations within one week of presentation.

2. Include Less Information
   - Limit presentations to 30 minutes.
   - Focus on immediate needs only.
   - Address future needs in follow-up (see sub-point 3 above).

3. Improve PowerPoint Expertise
   - Add zip (more colours, etc.).
   - Use fewer words and more illustrations.

   I think we do a good job already, but of course we could always do better.

   I'm looking forward to hearing what others have to say.

   Your Name

Mission Accomplished

1. You clearly state your purpose in the subject line.
2. You use the first-person point of view (I), because you are providing your own suggestions.
3. You acknowledge your familiarity with your reader by the ease of your opening statement.
4. You follow the general practice of providing three examples.
5. Your original headings were

   - better knowledge of customers' needs,
   - including too much, and
   - more training with the use of PowerPoint.

As you began to write from your outline, you noticed that the first and third headings signal an improvement, while the second signals a deficiency. For consistency, you reworded them. In your final version, all three read as recommendations for improvement, which is what you were asked to consider.

6. You reworked your supporting points so that they are more specific in detail and more immediately clear.
7. You changed the sequence of support in point 1 and made a connection between a similar point in 1 and 2. (Compare with outline on page 77.)

8. You decided to use two, not three, suggestions in 3.
9. You ensured that your lists are well-constructed and grammatically parallel (in this case, each item begins with a verb that complements the implied statement, "I suggest that we").
10. You closed on a note of confidence for your team and a positive expectation of hearing more good suggestions.
11. Your sentences are grammatically correct and clearly written.
12. The document is visually attractive.

MEMO
Scenario

You are the supervisor of a department with 23 staff members. Your single photocopier, which is leased, is constantly breaking down. It is clear that it cannot meet the demands that are being placed on it. You need to replace it with a better machine.

To accomplish this, you will need to write a memo to your manager, Curtis McArthur, who oversees four other departments in addition to yours. His office is located on another floor and generally you see him only at staff meetings. Productivity is his main goal, and he keeps a close eye on the budget, insisting on detailed backup before approving any changes to your operation.

Because of the urgency of the situation and the cost involved, you decide to write your request in memo format and leave it with Curtis's secretary. This form of delivery will be as fast as an e-mail, and more formal. You give yourself 30 minutes to complete this document.

Example

To: Curtis McArthur
From: Your Name
Date: May 15, 2008
Subject: Request for a New Photocopier

Our photocopier is inadequate for our needs and my department can't function without a replacement. Among its many problems, the following are the most critical:

- It has had 8 breakdowns in the last 2 months and 3 so far this month.
- It is way too slow at 15 copies/minute (we average 1500 copies/day).
- It lacks large format, magnification, and auto-feed features.

The copier is 6 years old and the repair technician says it's obsolete. No other department is using such an outdated copier.

He recommends we upgrade to Model 650 XSP. This will add $225/month, but sending the printing outside would cost double that and be extremely inconvenient.

They will adjust our contract as of the end of the month, so we'll be getting more than a week's use at the current rate.

The bottom line is that the constant breakdowns are affecting our productivity.

If you require more information, please let me know as soon as possible.

Your signature

Mission Accomplished

1. You clearly state your purpose in the subject line.
2. You use the first person plural point of view (*we*), because you are representing your department (and your company).
3. You state the urgency of your need in the first sentence.
4. You supply the level of detail you know your reader requires.
5. The details of the most critical faults are listed in order of importance.
6. You include the technician's assessment and a departmental comparison as two additional persuasive details.
7. Your document flows logically from problem description to solution.
8. You include the details of the additional cost.
9. You link breakdowns with loss of productivity in a concluding sentence to give your request maximum impact.
10. You invite the reader to make input but underline the urgency.
11. You ensure that your sentences are grammatically correct and clearly written.
12. You ensure that *it's* is spelled correctly.
13. You ensure that the document is visually attractive.

You took 5 minutes to plan, 20 minutes to write, and 5 minutes to revise your document. This did not include research time spent by your assistant.

LETTER
Scenario

You are a chartered accountant. Your new client, George Janovich, has submitted his income tax information to you on a spreadsheet that displays the revenue and expenditures for his wine importing business, which grossed $283,785 last year, his first year of business. Janovich was a referral from a long-time client of yours, who is excited by his friend's success and is considering getting into the wine business himself.

You note that while Janovich has included receipts for attendance at a Wine Expo in Rome in May and another in Argentina in August, there are no receipts for other expenses claimed as business travel to Paris and Australia. These total $9,437 for airfare, accommodation, and related expenses.

Another business expense is a wine cellar in his residence, built at a cost of $33,678. Knowing little about the wine business, you assume that this is where he temporarily stores his inventory before it is shipped out to customers. However, you wonder why he doesn't locate this storage space at his business address, for which he has provided receipts for lease of the property.

When you phone him for clarification, he tells you that he visited wine producers in Bordeaux and Australia and kept a record of his expenses but has misplaced the receipts. He says that if the tax authorities require receipts, he will "dig them up." Regarding the wine cellar in his residence, he says he is claiming it as a business expense because he often entertains clients in that room.

When you ask him to furnish more details about the nature of this activity, he says he has receipts for the design and installation of the cellar, but he hasn't kept a record of his client activity. He thought it would be obvious that someone in his line of work would have a legitimate business need for a first-class wine cellar.

You need to write a letter to Mr. Janovich, explaining why you cannot prepare a tax return showing these deductions unless he can provide travel receipts and sufficient detail to justify the claim that the wine cellar is a legitimate business expense.

You prefer to use the full block style of letter. You are self-employed and feel this adds a look of authority. The issues here are straightforward, but you do not want to offend Mr. Janovich. After all, he was referred by one of your long-term clients and this is your first time working with him. It is clear, however, that he has some misconceptions about claiming business expenses. You need to set the record straight. You give yourself 30 to 45 minutes to compose your letter.

Disclaimer: The following example is entirely fictitious and does not claim to contain accurate financial accounting advice.

Example

Your name, CGA
Blossom Accounting Services
55 Maitland Drive
Vancouver, BC V5Y 2Y6

March 22, 2008

Victor Jovanovich
1426 Forman Ave.
Vancouver, BC V9R 4S8

Dear Mr. Jovanovich:

RE: BUSINESS TAX FILING 2007

Further to our telephone conversation on March 20, I feel I should clarify the question of deductions for business expenses. I understand that visiting wine producers and maintaining a wine cellar are essential to your business. However, in each case a record of expenditures must be submitted, in accordance with Generally Accepted Accounting Principles (GAAP).

Business Travel Receipts
Both the tax authorities and GAAP require that all claims for travel expenditures be documented by receipts. This is particularly important should you be audited, as receipts provide evidence of your activities. You have provided receipts

(continued)

for your attendance at Wine Expos in Rome and Argentina, and so these expenses can be claimed. However, you must submit similarly detailed receipts for your travel to Bordeaux and Australia, or these expenses cannot be claimed.

Wine Cellar Expenses
Although you have kept receipts for the cost of design and installation of the cellar, it is unclear how it qualifies as a business expense. First, it is not located at your business address. If it were, and you could provide documentation for sustained business use (e.g., storage of presale wine), then the total cost could be amortized over 10 years.

Second, if you entertain clients in your wine cellar for a minimum of 15 hours per month, you can claim the cost of the wine (and food) served, but you must provide a record of activity (i.e., list of clients, date of visit, cost of wine consumed).

If you can locate these receipts, please send them to me immediately so that I can include them in your 2007 income tax filing.

Congratulations on a successful year in business, and I look forward to hearing from you soon.

If you have any further questions, please let me know.

Yours truly,

Your signature

Your Name, CA

Mission Accomplished

1. You clearly state your purpose in the subject line.
2. You choose full block format and ensure it is correct in every detail.

3. You use the second-person point of view (*you*), because you are addressing your comments to your client.

4. You make a connection with your previous telephone call.

5. You acknowledge the legitimate intent of your client's activities.

6. You tactfully state your purpose/main point in the first sentence.

7. You create appropriate headings.

8. You provide clear explanations and examples.

9. You use effective transitional words (*so, however, first, second*).

10. You ensure that your sentences are grammatically correct and clearly written.

11. You clearly state the action expected.

12. You end on a friendly note.

13. You ensure that your document is visually attractive.

PROPOSAL
Scenario

You are the executive director of an organization called School Is Life Alliance. In each of the past five years your organization has applied to the Tanaka Foundation for a community services grant. Your organization is well known for its integrity and effectiveness, and you have been approved for grants in three of these five years. Needs are great and money is scarce, however, and you cannot afford to rest on your reputation. The competition for the available funding increases every year. You know from experience that attempted solutions are unknowable until the many different pieces of a problem become evident, a process that can take a long time. Thus, recognizing the existence of a specific need is the first step in designing a program to address it.

A major responsibility in your position description is to secure funding wherever possible. Because of its importance to your organization, you choose not to delegate this responsibility. Thus, when the need for a particular project becomes clear, you assume the role of planning and writing the proposal.

The proposal shown below would take a full work day to write, assuming you had all the information in front of you. Although less than four pages long (see proposal formats, page 55), it is written not as a memo report but as a separate document, with cover letter, because it will be competing with other submissions for funding.

Example
Cover Letter

School Is Life Alliance
1234 Lakeshore Blvd. West
Toronto ON M6C 1G9
(647) 111-1111 • www.schoolislife.com

September 24, 2006

Ms. Shimina Farhad
Grants Officer
Tanaka Foundation
348 Trethway Avenue
London, ON R6A 5D5

Dear Ms. Farhad:

On behalf of the members of our alliance and the residents of Pleasant Park, I am pleased to forward the attached proposal requesting 2007 funding for a pre-school education program to be called When I Am Six.

Studies have shown that negative attitudes toward school based on the parents' own schooling experience can be transferred to their children as early as grade one. The primary objective of this proposal is to change that attitude by training 40 parent-mentors who can then mentor other parents. It is estimated that in any given year this would involve approximately 1,200 parent households and benefit 3,500 children. Although we are requesting funding for the first year only, we recommend that the program continue for a minimum of five years to ensure a sufficient baseline for the measurement of program goals.

The attached proposal outlines project goals, methodology, development, implementation, budget, and timeline. An evaluation report will be submitted in Week 50.

If you have any questions, or if there are omissions, please call me at 647-111-1111.

Yours truly,

Your Name

Director, School Is Life Alliance

Attachment: Tanaka Foundation Proposal

YN:bk

Proposal

Tanaka Foundation Proposal
2007 Grant Year

When I Am Six:
School Preparation for Families and Children in Pleasant Park
Submitted by School Is Life Alliance

Introduction

This proposal requests $67,500 for the development and implementation of a community-based program to assist with preparing parents and their pre-school children for the commencement of schooling at age six. Studies have shown that negative attitudes toward school based on the parents' own schooling experience can be transferred to their children as early as grade one.

The primary objective of this proposal is to change that attitude by training 40 parent-mentors who can then mentor other parents. It is estimated that in any given year this would involve approximately 1,200 parent households and benefit 3,500 children. It is recommended that the program continue for a minimum of five years to ensure a sufficient baseline for the measurement of program goals.

Program development would begin January 2, 2007, with implementation July 2.

School Is Life Alliance was founded in 2002 and is made up of a coalition of social agencies providing a broad range of services across the city.

Background

Pleasant Park has long been known as a challenging and complex neighbourhood. This is one of the poorest communities in the city, with over half the 12,000 residents under the age of 26 and a quarter of these (1,500) parents. The unemployment rate is 15 percent and close to half the children are living at the poverty level.

A 2005 survey revealed that while 90 percent of parents wanted their children to attend college or university, only 25

(continued)

percent thought this would be possible. Parents are angered that drugs and violence within their community are undermining their children's futures. Although several community-based agencies are doing their best to create an environment in which positive goals can be achieved, the process needs to begin much earlier and be focused on pre-school children and their parents.

During 2005, School Is Life laid the groundwork for the action outlined in this proposal by

- helping families in Pleasant Park understand the nature of the pre-school challenge;
- implementing the Safe Walk program to encourage attendance at after-school programs; and
- coordinating with other inner city agencies to encourage participation in summer indoor/outdoor educational and sport activities.

Proposed Plan

When I Am Six will create an effective pre-school education program for families and children that will ensure the greatest opportunity for success in education. The proposal is organized in two phases of six months each: program development and program implementation. An initial survey to all parents will determine eligibility and interest, as participation will be voluntary. In the second phase, trained parent-mentors will be assigned 20 to 30 parents each and will conduct one two-hour information session monthly for each half of their group.

Primary Objectives

- Reach into every voluntary household with children age five and below.
- Recruit and train parent-mentors who will inspire other parents in encouraging school preparedness within their families.
- Coordinate existing community resources to add voice.

Accessibility

- Offered free to all eligible families.

(continued)

- Led by parent-mentors from diverse cultures.
- Offered in safe locations within or near the community.

Key Benefits

Parents will benefit from increased understanding of

- the goals of primary education;
- the role of literacy and numeracy in their child's development;
- the importance of good nutrition;
- the relevance of play; and
- the importance of reading aloud to their children.

Children will benefit from all of the above and begin to imagine positive school experiences and include them in their conversations with their parents and playmates.

Budget

The request of $67,500 will cover program development for the first six months and implementation of the program for the second six months.

Development Phase: January 2–June 30, 2007

Item	Explanation	Cost
Coordinator	Organize program and community resources; hold information meetings; recruit and train parents; create survey and collate results; write report.	$21,500

(continued)

Development of Survey & Training Materials	Prepared by coordinator and community	In coordinator's job description
Printing of Survey and Training Materials	1,200 surveys; 40 sets of training materials	Surveys: $1,500 Materials: $500
Office Space Rental	Coordinator's space in community office	$600
Telephone; Fax		$300
TOTAL		$24,400

Implementation Phase: July 1–December 31, 2007

Item	Explanation	Cost
Parent-Mentors	40 @ $20/hr. 4 hrs/month for 6 months	$19,200
Coordinator	Oversight of program and mentor advisement	$21,500 (second half of salary)
Office Rental, Telephone & Fax		$900
Evaluation Survey	For inclusion in final report	$1,500
TOTAL		$43,100

(continued)

Timeline

Task	Responsibility	Completion Date
Formation of Steering Committee	Coalition agency partners	Week 2
Hiring of Coordinator	Steering committee	Week 4
Parent Survey Distribution	Coordinator	Week 8
Development of Training Program and Materials	Coordinator	Week 14
Recruitment of Parent-Mentors	Coordinator	Week 18
Training of Parent-Mentors	Coordinator	Week 22
Interim Report to Tanaka Foundation	Coordinator	Week 24
Program Implementation	Coordinator & Parent-Mentors	Week 25
Program Evaluation Survey	Coordinator	Week 48
Final Report	Coordinator & Parent-Mentors	Week 50

Submitted September 24, 2006
School Is Life Alliance
1234 Lakeshore Blvd. West
Toronto ON M6C 1G9
(647) 111-1111 • www.schoolislife.com

Mission Accomplished

1. Your cover letter uses letterhead block style and briefly summarizes the objective and content of the proposal. It also provides contact information. It is direct and clear.
2. Your introduction immediately states the amount of the request and restates the rationale provided in the covering letter. (This is a precaution since the two may become separated after submission.) The objective of the project is stated in the second paragraph and includes start and finish dates and the qualifications of your organization. (In this case, already known by the funding organization.)
3. You use the third-person point of view, because the subject is, variously, the proposal, the project, and the community.
4. The Background section includes context and brings the need into present-day focus.
5. The plan is logically presented, with three key subheadings followed by bulleted lists in support of each.
6. You ensure that your lists are correctly structured.
7. The budget is sequenced logically from largest to smallest expense and is clearly displayed in a table.
8. The timeline is sequential and clearly displayed in a table.

9. You ensure that your sentences are grammatically correct and clearly written.
10. You ensure that your document is visually attractive.

REPORT
Scenario

You are the VP Operations of Jet-Quik Courier Services. With a fleet of 20 courier vans and 8 cycle couriers who are under exclusive contract, Jet-Quik provides a broad range of courier services within the city of Vancouver, the North Shore, and Burnaby.

Your business has expanded since 1998 and last year's total revenue was $3.4 million. However, third-quarter results this year show a year-to-date loss of $193,000, mostly attributable to poor performance in three sectors of your business. The board has requested that a task group be formed to identify the reasons for the loss and make recommendations, including termination of some services, to ensure that this loss is not repeated. The president has asked you to lead the task group and submit a preliminary report as soon as possible.

You ask two senior management employees to join you in discussions and within two weeks you are ready to report your findings. Because this is a short report intended for internal distribution, you choose memo format. You dictate your report from outline notes, using voice-recognition software, then revise the headings and polish the text. This takes you approximately two hours, a task you complete on the weekend. Because of your senior position, you have the luxury of turning the report over to an assistant for page design and final proofreading.

Example

To:	Carlos DiMillo, President
From:	Your Name, Chair, Sector Task Group
	Peter Ling, Chief Accountant
	Niki Sioban, Manager, Business Development
Date:	December 16, 2005

Subject: Preliminary Report on Q3 Sector Losses

This report addresses revenue concerns in three sectors of our operation that have resulted in a loss of $193,000 YTD. On September 28, 2005, the Board requested that a Sector Task Group, under the direction of Richard Berg, coordinate an investigation into losses in the following sectors: Automotive Parts Delivery, Delayed Baggage Delivery, and Expedited Delivery. Findings and recommendations are based on financial analyses and interviews with sector managers.

Summary

Currently we serve a wide range of businesses: law firms and courthouses; medical labs and hospitals; financial institutions; automotive parts. With the exception of the legal sector, until last year our focus had been on scheduled delivery service. When this business contracted in 2003, we added delayed baggage delivery (DBD) and same-day expedited delivery (ED), the latter principally by bicycle courier. Although this increased our range of services, these sectors have not performed as expected and reassessment is required. Because of the state of the economy, Automotive Parts Delivery (APD) is also underperforming.

(continued)

The report recommends that we eliminate DBD and consolidate our other scheduled services. The report further recommends that we merge the medical and financial services fleets, seek new business, and both add and redeploy bicycle couriers.

Analysis
Automotive Parts Delivery

Q3   (64,000)
YTD   (97,000)

We have been providing four-hour scheduled deliveries daily, with two vans on two-hour alternating cycles in Zones A, B, and C. The past two quarters have seen a 35% downturn in the use of manufacturers' replacement parts and a corresponding loss of business. Efforts to secure contracts within the secondary market have not been successful. In September APD cut back to one van and redeployed the other to medical and second-day service, but it is underutilized. As a result, we have one driver and one van cruising at 40% utilization, resulting in the Q3 loss shown above.

Delayed Baggage Delivery

Q3   (49,000)
YTD   (73,000)

As the airlines have instituted checked-bag charges, fewer bags are being carried and therefore fewer bags are delayed arrivals. The DBD manager estimates that these are down at least 50% YTD. Contributing to the loss is the pricing schedule offered for competitive purposes when we secured these contracts. These are one-time deliveries anywhere within Zones A-C and should have been priced as ED service. Many are to apartment buildings, often necessitating long wait times until the owner appears. High volume increased the margin to an acceptable level, but current low volume means we will continue to operate at a loss.

Expedited Delivery

Q3   (8,000)
YTD   (23,000)

Since we already had five cycle couriers scheduled for downtown legal and financial deliveries, in March we took the

(continued)

opportunity to expand this sector of the business to include patient records, digital media, inter-office mail, etc. In May we rolled out a guaranteed mission-critical service level of 30 minutes in Zone A, which has proven to be very successful. However, this has caused some delivery delays in the legal and financial sectors and subsequent loss of business. Attempts to hire experienced cycle couriers to meet this growth have been unsuccessful. If we are unable to find a way around this, we may have to refocus this sector.

Recommendations
Immediate

1. Maintain APD at current level of service with one van.
2. Place one driver on temporary layoff.
3. Redeploy three of our five bicycle couriers to full-time 30-minute service and replace them with couriers of less experience (an apprenticeship model).

End Q4

1. Terminate Delayed Baggage Delivery at end of contract and reassign manager.
2. Place a second driver on temporary layoff.

Opportunities

1. Grow our medical delivery business. Aging demographic and the increase in private clinics and labs present significant opportunities for new contracts.
2. Merge medical delivery with financial document sector operations to realize economy of scale and more efficient utilization of scheduled fleet services.

These recommendations are based on preliminary investigation and warrant further discussion.

Mission Accomplished

1. As this report is in memorandum format, you use a subject line to state its focus.

2. You use *we* as your point of view, because you are reporting your findings and recommendations on behalf of the company.

3. You do not use *Introduction* as a heading. Instead, you begin by stating the purpose of the report and who requested it. Under *Summary*, you provide the context and summarize the recommendations.

4. In the discussion section, which you choose to head *Analysis*, you briefly analyze each of the sectors, at the outset indicating the losses in Q3 and YTD.

5. With each analysis you describe the operation of the particular service and the attempts made to improve it. You include relevant dates, statistics, and conclusions.

6. Your sentences are clear yet detailed throughout.

7. Note that you use the % sign, a common practice in business documents.

8. You use conjunctions (*however, if, although*) throughout to indicate the nature of relationships.

9. Recommendations follow the analysis section and are structured accurately and listed below three time-based headings.
10. The report ends with an action statement (*further discussion is warranted*).
11. You ensure that your document is visually attractive.

MINUTES
Scenario

The following example represents the minutes of the discussion that led to the *When I Am Six* proposal. In this meeting you are the Youth Services Counsellor at Pleasant Park Community Centre. It is your turn to record the minutes, write them up, and ensure that they are distributed by e-mail. You have done this several times before and the others have complimented you on your ability to express the main points concisely while still capturing the flow and spirit of the discussion.

Example

<table>
<tr><td colspan="2"></td><td colspan="2" align="right">Minutes of Meeting</td></tr>
<tr><td>Minutes No.:</td><td>029</td><td>Ref.:</td><td>12-08-07-008</td></tr>
<tr><td>Prepared by:</td><td>Shirley Young</td><td>Date:</td><td>August 19, 2006</td></tr>
<tr><td>Meeting date:</td><td>August 12, 2006</td><td>Time:</td><td>9:00 AM</td></tr>
<tr><td>Location:</td><td>244 Connelly Dr.</td><td>Project:</td><td></td></tr>
<tr><td>Subject:</td><td colspan="3">Tanaka Foundation Draft Proposal</td></tr>
</table>

Present:

School Is Life	Amanda Leger (AL)	Director
Pleasant Park Community Centre	Shirley Young (SY)	Youth Services Counsellor
Plaxton Hall	Pernilla Astrid (PA)	Pre-school Counsellor
St. Benedict's	Estavo Safarin (ES)	Director

Distribution:	All Present Including:	
	Samuel Nkono, PPCC	Manager Accounting
	Ishmay Vincent, PPCC	Manager Day Care
	Transmitted via E-Mail	

MINUTES

Point No.	Description	Action by	Date
1.0 1.1	**PROPOSAL OBJECTIVES** AL described the project, which will prepare children age 1-5 for entrance into kindergarten, and requested input from the group. She circulated a preliminary list of objectives. After discussion, the list was reduced to three: contact volunteer households with children below age 7; recruit parent-mentors to encourage school preparation in families; coordinate existing community resources to assist. SY and PA offered to help with a family recruitment survey.		
2.0 2.1	**PLAN DETAILS** The proposal is asking for $67,550 and will have two six-month phases, development and implementation. A full-time co-ordinator needs to be hired, a survey developed, and 40 parent-mentors recruited and trained. Start date	AL, ES, PA	12/09

	January 2, 2007. ES and PA will assist AL in writing up a job description. They can also refer some potential candidates.		
2.2	Coordinator will oversee entire project from start to finish. Training materials will be developed in first six months, and mentors selected and trained to begin June 15.		
2.3	Program will be free to participating families, who will receive guidance for one two-hour period per month, with follow-up visits from the mentor. Mentors will represent the cultural diversity of the neighbourhood. SY suggested that some of the mentors could be fathers and AL will note this in the proposal.	AL	
2.4	ES recommended that the benefits be listed in the proposal. SY and PA suggested that importance of nutrition and relevance of play be included.		
2.5	It was agreed that the main goal of the project is to create a positive image of school from the very first year and to encourage conversation between parents and their children that makes completing school a worthwhile and achievable goal.		
3.0	**BUDGET** Major expenses are coordinator's salary and payment to parent-mentors. ES and PA stated that $43,000 was fair and necessary to get a qualified person. There was discussion whether paying mentors $20/hr. was too much, but it was agreed that since they are only paid for 4 hours/month and asked to do follow-up, it is actually less than this. SY said she could provide an office. AL said the surveys might cost less than budgeted, leaving some $ for contingencies.		
4.0	**TIMELINE** All present volunteered to sit on the Steering Committee, headed by AL, with first meeting on September 12. Proposal applicants will be notified by November 1. If successful, coordinator must be hired by end of January. AL will circulate the completed timeline before the next meeting.	AL	
	OTHER BUSINESS There being no further business, the meeting adjourned at 10:50 a.m.		
	If there are any errors or omissions, please contact: Shirley Young, 416-111-1111 ext. 222 shirley@schoolislife.com		

Mission Accomplished

1. Your headings clearly reflect the purpose of the meeting, which was to receive feedback on the draft proposal.
2. Your numbering system follows the sequence of discussion.
3. You numbered each heading and sub-point for clarity and future reference.
4. Your sentences are simple and direct.
5. You include conclusions only; you exclude the debate leading to them.
6. Your content is detailed and well organized.
7. You report the main points of the discussion in an objective way.
8. You ensure accuracy of grammar and spelling.
9. You are meticulous in conforming to the format.

ANSWERS TO SELF-TEST QUESTIONS

FEEDBACK ON PENCIL SHARPENER INSTRUCTIONS, PAGES 37–8

These instructions are obviously written at a very basic level, as if addressed to a child. However, a child is not likely to be the purchaser, and therefore we must assume that they were written to be read by adults.

I think you will agree that adult readers would find the following to be sufficient:

Insert the pencil into the sharpening hole and firmly press downward. Remove after a few seconds. Slide out the shavings tray to empty it.

SELF-TEST 1 (PAGE 110)

1. If a window in the shape of a rectangle capped by a semi-circle has a perimeter of 24 feet, *what* dimensions should the architect choose for each shape in order to admit the greatest amount of light?

2. The market for hand-painted wood figurines is strong, *and therefore* we are hiring more staff.

   The market for hand-painted wood figurines is strong. *Therefore*, we are hiring more staff.

3. To meet demand, *we have hired* 14 new staff and *enlarged* the plant.

4. *Three companies* have met the tender deadline.

5. *We have hired a consultant* to improve our public relations.

6. In my position with Galileo Aerospace *I also had clearance to handle classified information.*

7. The *marketing department* [you know its role so an explanation doesn't have to be included] *has been relocated* to the east wing in order to be closer to the Senior Management team.

   The marketing department has been relocated to the east wing. *This move will provide faster access* [if you want to include this] for media relations planning sessions with Senior Management.

8. We were planning to complete the audit by the end of the week. *However*, we have not been able to obtain all the necessary information.

   We were planning to complete the audit by the end of the week, but we have not been able to obtain all the necessary information.

9. *Because we derive* most of our revenue from subscriptions, we are aggressively seeking to expand this base.

We derive most of our revenue from subscriptions, *and therefore* we are aggressively seeking to expand this base.

10. In 2008 the financial industry in North America lost a total of $1.2 trillion. *The industry may take years* to recover from *this loss.*

In 2008 the financial industry in North America lost a total of $1.2 trillion. *The North American economy* may take years to recover from *this setback.*

SELF-TEST 2 (PAGES 146–7)

1. This report *provides* information that management feels is relevant to recent decisions.
2. If our final quarter's results *came* in as expected, we would surpass last year's record total revenue.
3. Half our business is generated in New Haven, and the other *half is generated* in Copenhagen. (OR We generate half in NH and half in C.)
4. The entire staff *are* concerned, but they are afraid to speak up.
5. *We started* our business here in 2002.
6. The new sales manager is friendly, smart, and *enthusiastic.*
7. The three admin staff chosen *were* Nika Rasky, Rami Faroud, and Emily Fong.

8. Neither of the two *is* suitable.
9. *I believe* (OR I think) that next year will show a positive return on investment.
10. The rising cost of raw materials *has* forced us to seek cheaper alternatives.

SELF-TEST 3 (PAGE 157)

1. X costs *more than* Y.
2. *If the job* can be performed in-house, *it is less expensive* than sending it out.
3. *Because* the shipment of servers has been delayed, next week's training session *is postponed.*

   Because the shipment of servers has been delayed, the training session will be held April 15 at the same time and place.
4. A consistent pattern of micromanagement tells employees that *management* doesn't trust their work or judgement.
5. *Please consider combining* the two departments.

INDEX